FEMINISM AND POP CULTURE

Published by
Seal Press
A Member of Perseus Books Group
1700 Fourth Street
Berkeley, California

10 9 8 7 6 5 4 3 2

Library of Congress Cataloging-in-Publication Data

Zeisler, Andi, 1972-
  Feminism and pop culture / Andi Zeisler.
    p. cm. -- (Seal studies)
  ISBN-13: 978-1-58005-237-5
  ISBN-10: 1-58005-237-1
  1. Feminism--United States. 2. Popular culture--United States. I.
Title.
  HQ1421.Z45 2008
  305.420973'09045--dc22

                                    2008019056

Cover design by Kate Basart, Union Pageworks
Cover illustration © Lauren Simkin Berke c/o rileyillustration.com
Interior design by Michael Walters
Printed in the United States of America
Distributed by Publishers Group West

FEMINISM AND POP CULTURE

ANDI ZEISLER

SEAL
Studies

For my first and favorite MTV-watching partner:
my father

CONTENTS

PROLOGUE

MY NAME IS ANDI, and I'm a pop cultureholic. I subscribe to twelve different magazines and have piles and piles more gathering dust in various parts of my house. I have elaborate plans to someday make sense of the hundreds of books and CDs I own, but for now they sit on shelves and in storage receptacles crying out for order. I have a uselessly encyclopedic memory for bands, album and song titles, and lyrics that came about because I spent much of my first two years of high school hiding out in the library and reading back issues of *Rolling Stone*. My computer brims with podcasts and blogs that would require eleven more hours in each day to keep up with, but even if I had those extra eleven hours I'd likely spend at least eight of them watching TV.

I'm lucky, however, because I can legitimately say that keeping up with popular culture is my job. Twelve years ago, I cofounded *Bitch: Feminist Response to Pop Culture* with my high school friend and fellow pop junkie Lisa Jervis. Lisa and I were both obsessed with how women were represented in pop culture. On every channel, in every magazine, in every darkened movie theater, we saw the way pop culture limited women's roles—they were girlfriends and victims, hookers and corpses, sex bombs and cock teases—and we wanted to talk about why. As ardent feminists and voracious readers, we were primed to dig into some analysis of how feminism had affected pop culture and vice versa, but apart from some deeply academic (and thus somewhat inscrutable) papers and books, we couldn't find much. And so we decided to write our own. We started *Bitch* as a zine in which our love of pop culture and our dedication to feminism could mingle, and in the process we tried to reframe pop culture: No longer a guilty feminist pleasure, it could be a locus of activism. We wanted to talk about why women rarely appeared on the covers of *Rolling Stone* or *Spin* and why, when they did, they were invariably missing most of their clothes. We wanted to talk about why daytime talk shows treat teen girls pursuing sexual pleasure as a problem to be contained. We wanted to talk about why the unisex Big Wheels of our youth had been replaced at the toy store by gender-specific pink "Princess Coaches" and blue "Rough Riders." We wanted to talk about the fact that pop culture was not just the fluff that came over the airwaves and through the newsstands but rather was the material from which young people's impressions of their world are molded.

I'm not totally sure when pop culture took over a significant chunk of my own social education, but I do know that, as for many women, my discovery of what I came to know as feminism was sparked by pop culture—pop culture involving Burt Reynolds, to get embarrassingly specific. I have no idea what I was watching around the age of seven—a TV show? a movie?—but the image that shocked and enraged my young self was that of Mr. Reynolds entering a bathroom in which a woman was showering, popping his head behind the shower curtain, and snapping a photo of the unsuspecting lady. Folks, I was livid. At an age when nothing seems more private than nudity, and nothing more undignified than having that nudity exposed, I wanted to hunt down Burt Reynolds on behalf of that showering gal and kick him in the shins, repeatedly. It would be years before I read texts and novels that articulated the pain and powerlessness women experience from sexual harassment and assault—works such as Susan Brownmiller's *Against Our Will* and Toni Morrison's *The Bluest Eye*—but in that moment I was ready to start fighting so that no woman would ever again have to know the violation of being surprised in the shower with a flashbulb.

Through my years editing *Bitch*, speaking at colleges, and talking with fellow pop-loving feminists, I've heard many stories in which a girl's simmering anger at being catcalled on the street, belittled by a male teacher, or simply made to feel like "just" a girl was later made clearer through a snippet of film dialogue or a passage in a book. Popular culture has become our common language, and to become fluent in it is, like it or not, a key part of making sense of the larger world. Pop culture is also a key route to making the concept of feminism—which still manages to send many women and men into a kind of nervous tizzy—both resonant and relatable. Perhaps the most gratifying part of my work has been seeing others make connections between popular culture's representations of women and girls and the need for feminism—not as a lofty, highfalutin, political movement but as a part of everyday life. I regularly read letters from high school girls saying things like, "You know, I thought I was the only one bothered by [name of TV show or movie], but I'm so happy to know I'm not alone," and from adult women and men saying they're happy to have a way to talk with their daughters about sexism in a contemporary context. Letters such as these are the best proof that offering a feminist critique of pop culture is, unfortunately, a job that still needs doing.

In outlining the long and often contentious relationship between feminism and pop culture, this book only scratches the surface of its history. There are places where I'm sure I've left out something important or defining. So if you, like me, are a book-collecting, magazine-subscribing, TV-obsessed, feminist pop omnivore, I probably don't need to tell you to look at this book as just the start.

CHAPTER 1

POP AND CIRCUMSTANCE: WHY POP CULTURE MATTERS

So: Pop Culture. Let's Define It.

Actually, this is quite a bit easier said than done. Definitions of popular culture depend on who's defining it and what his or her agenda is. In a purely literal sense, popular culture is any cultural product that has a mass audience. In Shakespeare's time, it was the theater. In ours, it's everything from Top 40 radio to *The Simpsons* to Paris Hilton. But historically, pop culture grew out of low culture, the uncouth counterpart to so-called high culture. If high culture comprised the art, literature, and classical music made by and for the world's educated elite, low culture was the baser stuff with which the masses contented themselves. As the phrase "pop culture" gradually came to take the place of "low culture," it was defined more by what it wasn't—elegant, refined, erudite—than by what it was. Mass culture that supposedly engaged the prurient interests and visceral (rather than cerebral) urges of people assumed to be ill educated and unworthy of "real" art. Museum exhibits were high culture, comic books were low; literature was high culture, pulp magazines and novels were low. As the Marxist literary critic Walter Benjamin wrote in his famous essay "The Work of Art in the Age of Mechanical Reproduction," "The masses seek distraction whereas art demands concentration from the spectator." High art was supposed to entertain, yes, but it was also supposed to inform, enrich, and inspire. It was considered enough, however, for popular culture to simply amuse.

Thus pop culture came to be understood—and, by many, looked down upon—as that which entertains masses of people by "distracting" them and by calling on their common references. ("Entertaining," of course, is a subjective word: I, personally, am not entertained by Sylvester Stallone movies, but even though I've never sat through the entire length of one of them I cannot deny knowing the names of at least eight. Why? Because Mr. Stallone's oeuvre entertains enough other people that his movies have become part of a lexicon of our culture.)

The economics of pop culture further complicates defining it. Popular culture is available to anyone with the money to access it. In Shakespeare's time, that meant a sausage merchant might take in a performance alongside an aristocrat if both bought a ticket. These days, the symphony is still considered high culture—but what about symphonies that give free concerts in public parks attended by people who drink beer to the rarefied strains of Dvořák? We pay to consume pop culture: $10 for a movie ticket, $17.95 for a CD, $4.95 for a magazine, $75 for a Broadway play, $50 per month for cable TV and Internet access. But we're also sold *to* popular culture via its dependence on advertising. Advertising didn't come along, after all, because producers of radio broadcasts and television programs decided they wanted to break up an hour by telling listeners and viewers about products they could buy; those broadcasts and programs existed so advertisers had an easy vehicle with which to peddle their wares.

This book focuses on American pop culture, so it makes sense to point out here that the United States—while obviously not the only nation that produces pop culture—leads the world in its export. Pop culture has replaced more tangible products as the United States' biggest export, and as countries such as India, Malaysia, and Russia have replaced state-owned broadcasting channels with those that are privately owned, our cultural reach into other continents has deepened. Even ill-gotten American pop culture is flourishing abroad—the growth of both technology and piracy worldwide has led to a booming trade in illegal DVD sales and unlicensed movie broadcasts.

Our pop products—from Mickey Mouse to Michael Jackson to Levi's—are cultural, and sometimes literal, currency in other countries. But the things the United States is selling so cheaply to these new capitalist markets aren't necessarily our best efforts. It can be disheartening to hear that a show such as *Baywatch* is the most-watched TV show the world over, or that girls in Fiji—a nation that has historically prized plump bodies—began suffering from eating disorders shortly after the island nation introduced U.S. television in 1995. But such information also reinforces the idea that pop culture, entertainment or not, is absolutely crucial to how people understand and live in the world. It may be just as critical in shaping societies as the more prestigious offerings of high culture.

So What Are We Talking About When We Talk About Pop Culture?

Well, we're talking about television. We're talking about movies. We're talking about radio. We're talking about MTV, NBC, BET, VH1, and HBO. We're talking about websites and LiveJournals and sports radio. We're talking about fashion magazines and celebrity tabloids. We're talking about board games such as Clue and Monopoly, toys such as Barbie and Bratz, online pursuits such as Doom and Second Life.

We're also talking about things that were in no way created to entertain us but that nevertheless become part of our mass consciousness: social and political events that stand as touchstones of collective experience—the Vietnam War, the impeachment hearings of President Clinton, the horrors of 9/11 and Hurricane Katrina—as well as coverage of these events on daytime talk shows, nightly news, and everything in between. As we talk about these events—and dissect the meaning of how others talk about them—those very conversations become pieces of popular culture: Think Anderson Cooper's excoriation of FEMA during Hurricane Katrina, or Jerry Falwell's assertion that "the pagans, and the abortionists, and the feminists, and the gays and the lesbians" were responsible for the terrorist attacks of 9/11.

And we're talking about the commercial forces that inspire and encourage us to open our wallets in pursuit of visceral pleasure, personal expression, and group identity—the beauty advertising that tells us that a certain foundation will imbue us with confidence, the car commercial that appeals to our hedonism, the sneakers that are deliberately marketed to us so that we'll feel stronger and healthier every time we lace them up. Advertising has long been an aspect of pop culture whose focus is deliberately on women. Soap operas, for instance, got their name from the detergent manufacturers such as Procter & Gamble that created episodic melodramas that were broadcast on radio during the day, when housewives were most likely to be listening.

We're also talking about the way we understand both the time and place in which we live and the way we define ourselves as individuals. When we look at our lives—both personally and collectively—we view them largely through the lens of popular culture, using songs, slogans, ad jingles, and television shows as shorthand for what happened at the time and how we experienced it. When we see a short film in which the Doors song "The End" plays over a black-and-white clip of soldiers in uniform, we understand it as a reference to the Vietnam War, because the Doors were a popular band during the years in which that war took place. That same clip updated to 2006 and accompanied by a song off the Green Day CD *American Idiot* would just as readily be understood as a reference to the war in Iraq.

And this is why pop culture can never be dismissed as being "just" about entertainment. Take the Vietnam War example: In the late 1960s and early 1970s, rock, folk, and experimental music were some of the chief expressions of an entire generation's disillusionment with what it saw as a pointless war waged by a repressive, hypocritical government. The music was entertaining in that it was pleasing to the ear, the performers were interesting to look at, and the experience of it was often enhanced by drugs. But the music was also a social statement, and it resonated not only with the people who were making it and hearing it then but with people of later generations who heard it and found that they, too, were moved by the melodies, the lyrics, and the emotions contained within. The same can be said for music that came out of specific cultural communities—hip-hop in the 1980s, for instance, or Riot Grrrl in the 1990s. Each form had its own reasons for existing beyond simply providing the pleasure of hearing and seeing it, and it's impossible to talk about the music without acknowledging those reasons.

As it happens, the barrier that once existed between high culture and low culture has been whittled away to the thinnest of shards, and the voices that once conferred status on one form over another have become so many and so diverse that they often drown each other out. Shakespeare, Homer, and Dickens were the low culture of their respective eras, yet because of the vagaries of time are considered high culture in ours. Comic books, once derided as pabulum for kids and illiterate adults, have become the subject of retrospectives in major art museums. And television, movies, and music have become fodder for the realm of "cultural studies" at colleges and universities.

Cultural studies is the all-purpose umbrella term for the interdisciplinary examination of a phenomenon or phenomena—a groundbreaking novel, a record-breaking film, an icon such as Michael Jordan—in the context of its social value, influence, and ideology. It's usually informed by sociology, anthropology, literary theory, political science, and race and gender studies. You may be studying it right now. In any case, the rise of cultural studies—which might encompass anything from African American film theory to Jewish American humor in literature to Madonna studies—has further chipped away at the distinctions between high and low (after all, if you can study it in college, it can't be too trashy, right?) and made pop culture both past and present an increasingly rich source of fodder for examination and analysis. We are, in the words of Walter Benjamin, still seeking distraction, but pop culture these days seems to demand the concentration he proposed to be the domain of high-art spectators. And it gets it: These days, newspapers such as the *New York Times* cover TV and blogs with a relish that would have been unthinkable even two decades ago. Most media provide far more space for reviewing television shows than for reviewing literature. And even those who create high art—painters, sculptors, installation makers—use tools of and references to mass culture for inspiration.

So What's This Book About?

The subject of this book is feminism and pop culture, and it tackles two sides of that topic: first, how popular culture has inspired, fueled, and furthered the women's movement and feminism; and second, how feminism has been depicted in popular culture. In the most general sense, the aim of this book is to provide a survey of the way feminism has interacted with popular culture as both catalyst and subject.

In the past decade or two, feminism and popular culture have become more closely entwined than ever before. This can in part be chalked up to the growing interest in cultural studies as an academic discipline and the resulting number of academic papers, conferences, and books devoted to feminist analyses of various facets of pop. (The field of studies devoted to *Buffy the Vampire Slayer* alone is proof that feminist cultural studies is no passing fad.) But it can also be explained by the fact that, well, there's a whole lot more popular culture to watch, read, examine, and deconstruct. Television networks are continually expanding their programming slates, and many in the past few years have switched to a year-round programming schedule that makes the phrase "summer rerun" nearly obsolete. Print magazines such as *Bust*, *Entertainment Weekly*, *Radar*, and *Bitch* are interested in pop culture as common language and as genuine pleasure. And the Internet teems with blogs, e-zines, and social-networking sites that not only dissect existing pop culture but create their own.

There are feminist issues that seem, it's true, more immediately vital than whether TV or movie characters are reflecting the lives of real women. There are the continuing problems of the gap between men's and women's wages, of glass ceilings and tacit sex discrimination in the workplace. There is the need to combat violence against girls and women and promote sexual autonomy. There are ongoing battles, both individual and collective, against limiting cultural definitions of "mother" and "wife." There's the fact that the Equal Rights Amendment, first proposed in 1923, has as of this writing still not been ratified by the United States Congress—meaning that under the U.S. Constitution women are not equal to men. And there are even broader, more global, and more complex issues of what it means to be a woman, a feminist, and a seeker of human and civil rights. But like the disintegrating line between high and low culture, the distinctions between political and pop have also all but disappeared. Pop culture informs our understanding of political issues that on first glance seem to have nothing to do with pop culture; it also makes us see how something meant as pure entertainment can have everything to do with politics.

I first heard the term "male gaze" in high school, and it sent me back to my seven-year-old self, watching Burt Reynolds watch that naked woman in the shower. I got angry all over again. It seems that for many women, a formative experience with that uncomfortable gaze—maybe in an issue of *Playboy*, maybe in an oil painting in a museum—becomes a defining moment. The male gaze affects how women view pop culture and how we view ourselves. And the concept of the male gaze itself is one that's crucial to understanding why reforming and reframing popular culture is a feminist project.

What is the male gaze? Put simply, it's the idea that when we look at images in art or on screen, we're seeing them as a man might—even if we are women—because those images are constructed to be seen by men. John Berger's 1972 fine-art monograph *Ways of Seeing* didn't coin the phrase, but it did describe the gendered nature of looking this way: "*Men act* and *women appear*. Men look at women. Women watch themselves being looked at. This determines not only most relations between men and women but also the relation of women to themselves. The surveyor of women in herself is male: the surveyed female. Thus she turns herself into an object—and most particularly an object of vision: a sight."

A year or two later, Laura Mulvey took this concept further in what's become a well-known work of psychoanalytic film theory, "Visual Pleasure and Narrative Cinema." In talking about the way narrative film reinforces the gender of the film's viewer using a sequence of "looks,"

© Getty Images

Ah, the male gaze. It's the idea that women are portrayed in art, in advertising, and on screen from a man's point of view, as objects to be looked at. Here, photographer Nick Bruno photographs a model in his studio.

Mulvey drew on Freudian psychoanalysis. She wrote that the male unconscious, which, according to Freud's theories, is consumed with a fear of castration, deals with that fear by seeking power over women, who represent the castrating figure. So by positioning women as nothing more than objects to be looked at, sexualized, and made vulnerable, the male unconscious reassures itself that, really, it has nothing to fear from women. As Mulvey put it:

> In a world ordered by sexual imbalance, pleasure in looking has been split between active/male and passive/female. The determining male gaze projects its phantasy on to the female figure which is styled accordingly. In their traditional exhibitionist role women are simultaneously looked at and displayed, with their appearance coded for strong visual and erotic impact so that they can be said to connote to-be-looked-at-ness. Woman displayed as sexual object is the leit-motif of erotic spectacle: from pin-ups to strip-tease, from Ziegfeld to Busby Berkeley she holds the look, plays to and signifies male desire.

Despite the clunkiness of the phrase "to-be-looked-at-ness," Mulvey pinpointed the way that images of women onscreen (and, by extension, on television, in magazines, on billboards . . .) seek to align viewers of any gender with the male gaze. So it makes sense that many girls and women grow up seeing images of girls and women the way men do—the images themselves are simply constructed that way. The mother figure is sexless; the cheerleader is hypersexual. The girl alone in her house is a potential victim, the man coming to the door an obvious rapist. Seeing the visual cues of the male gaze, in turn, affects how women understand images of other women on screen.

What "Visual Pleasure and Narrative Cinema" didn't suggest, however, is that perhaps there is a corresponding female gaze that informs how women see images of both themselves and of men and affects the images they themselves create. This, of course, had largely to do with the fact that female screenwriters and directors were few and far between at the time Mulvey was writing—and, in many places, remain so. Since the 1975 publication of Mulvey's article, feminist and cultural critics have responded to it—both directly and indirectly—with essays and books that attempt to define a female gaze and parse the many ways in which images of women can be claimed as powerful and even subversive. And many more authors, filmmakers, musicians, and artists have made work that takes on the male gaze directly, flipping the script on the likes of Berger and Mulvey with imagery that is unsettling in its confrontation of the looker.

Television was, for most women, the first place they saw themselves represented. And for a long time, they didn't see much besides loving wives, dutiful daughters, gossiping girlfriends, fashion plates, and the occasional dowdy maid, nanny, or granny. The same went for magazines and books. In *Where the Girls Are: Growing Up Female with the Mass Media*, author Susan J. Douglas wrote of postwar pop culture and feminism, "Here's the contradiction we confront: the news media, TV shows, magazines, and films of the past four decades may have turned feminism into a dirty word, but they also made feminism inevitable." Without pop culture's limited images of women, many actual women in the real world might not have been inspired to fight for more and better representations of themselves.

From the start of the modern women's liberation movement (not to be confused with the so-called first wave of feminism, or the suffrage

What's Your Worst Memory of Women in Pop Culture?

"There's an episode of M*A*S*H where the guys rig the shower tent, so when it collapses suddenly while Hot Lips, the only woman, is showering, all the guys are on lawn chairs and snacking on popcorn, enjoying the show. It's played for major sitcom laughs. I saw this when I was about twelve. I wish I could say I was horrified when I saw the way the show represented the body of the only major female character, but I wasn't. I didn't laugh, either. I was simply confused. I suppose this is when I began to see how female bodies were treated as public property in a way that men's bodies weren't." —Anna

"When I was growing up, I was a real tomboy—I dreamed of joining the Army or a street gang or a rock band, wore tough muscle tees, cropped my hair, etc. (I totally sucked at sports, but for some reason this didn't deter me.) As a result, I had all kinds of pop culture dissonances going on—it was the late '70s. You can imagine. For some reason, one thing that really got to me was the host on Family Feud, Richard Dawson. He was really oily and would always kiss all of the lady guests. I had this fantasy of going on the show in this Georgia Bulldogs shirt that I owned and refusing to kiss him when he approached me. Somehow, this seemed highly symbolic to me. I would mentally rehearse various ways of rejecting him, up to and including popping him in the nose." —Jessica

"I really wanted to watch the movie The Hotel New Hampshire because I had a huge crush on Rob Lowe. So my friend and I rented it. What I didn't know was that the movie also had this awful scene where Jodie Foster's character is gang-raped in the woods by a bunch of guys from her school. There was a lot of thrusting, and it was just awful. I went home feeling sick to my stomach, and then I couldn't even talk to my parents about what was bothering me because saying I had seen a rape scene was too embarrassing—I associated it with sex, and I didn't want them to know I thought about sex. I have still never seen The Accused because I can't watch Jodie Foster be raped again." —Donna

"I saw the movie Grease with my best friend and her parents when I was, I don't know, ten maybe. I loved it, and my friend and I got the record soon after and sang along to it all the time. As a city girl, it struck me really hard that there wasn't one black person in it—that led to a long conversation with *my friend's parents afterward about segregation. So that was one thing. But the sexual stuff was kind of nuts, and I'm embarrassed now to think about my friend and I singing, 'Look at me, I'm Sandra Dee/Lousy with virginity' and not knowing what the hell it meant. Our parents must have been dying. I've seen it several times since and wonder how many girls internalized the whole Sandy versus Rizzo, virgin-whore thing. I know I did.* Grease *wasn't the only reason, but I'm sure it had a lot to do with forming my friends' and my perception of how we appealed to guys."* —April

"The thing that comes to mind is the day that Mattel announced that the 'New Barbie' had been released, and if you came to the toy store with your old Barbie and turned her in, you got a discount on the New Barbie. I waited in line with my mom for a long time, in a snake line of moms and little girls. And finally they took my old Barbie, with her perfect ponytail and striped swimsuit and high-heeled mules, and gave me . . . an abomination! I hated New Barbie. Even at age six I could tell she looked cheap. Her face was hard, not delicate, her skin was sticky and semi-soft, instead of hard plastic. Her breasts were too big. She didn't have painted toenails. She had holes in the bottoms of her arches. She didn't have blue eye shadow painted on her lids. And worst of all, her hair was like brown dental floss—it was shiny, but icky, not like the beloved, soft ponytail on old Barbie that I loved to pet. I had to cut it all off, and then she had bald spots. Decades later, I still felt such bitterness over this that when Mattel offered a collectors' edition of Barbie, I bought her. And some little kid visiting our house stole her sunglasses the first day I brought her home. People just can't keep fucking around with Barbie. I never believed in 'new and improved' again." —Susie

"I watched part of the 'crime-scene corpse' episode of America's Next Top Model *where the models were challenged to pose as sexy murder victims—covered with bruises, bloody, broken-looking, in come-hither clothing and vampy makeup. Some of them looked like victims of domestic violence; some looked like they'd been raped. And the celebrity judges looked at the pictures and they were all, 'Ooh, you look so beautiful and dead in this one! I love the broken leg and the bruises! Sexy! Gorgeous!' One of the models had lost a close friend to a drug overdose before the episode was shot, and she was complimented on how well she did during her session (in which she posed as a very glamorous strangling victim). A small piece of my soul crumbles away when I think of it. I get so tired of seeing sexy dead women."* —Anne

movement), its most successful members understood that activism doesn't happen in a vacuum and that in order to make change, it's often necessary to put idealism in the most understandable context. For many people, that context is the popular culture that's consumed as entertainment. So it's probably no accident that some of the highest-profile actions of the second wave movement involved popular culture. There was the 1968 protest in Atlantic City of the Miss America Pageant; a 1970 sit-in at the offices of prescriptive women's magazine *Ladies' Home Journal*; a "nude-in" held at Grinnell College in 1969 to protest a speech by a representative of *Playboy*. Each of these demonstrations made the case that pop culture matters, and that dismantling such pop products—or remaking them to reflect real women's lives—was an imperative part of women's liberation. As Douglas wrote, "[I]f enough people think studying the media is a waste of time, then the media themselves can seem less influential than they really are. Then they get off the hook for doing what they do best: promoting a white, upper–middle-class, male view of the world." Feminism is full of unfinished projects, and liberating pop culture from the male gaze is just one. As we'll see throughout this book, it continues today in myriad ways.

The Commerce Connection

In examining how feminism has informed pop culture and vice versa, it's instructive to look at the way the evolution of the women's movement has been mirrored in pockets of popular culture. This evolution has almost never been linear; as with women's experiences as a whole, many representations of women in pop culture have stayed stubbornly behind the curve of liberation expectations. But others have changed with the times, alternately gratifying and frustrating the women who watch carefully, looking for accurate portrayals of who they are and can be.

In 1970s pop culture, for example, women were no longer just playing the role of the sweet, pliant housewife. They were going to work (*The Mary Tyler Moore Show*), getting divorced (*An Unmarried Woman*), having abortions (*Maude*), standing up for injustice (*Norma Rae*), and rocking hard (bands such as Heart and Fanny). They were also talking to each other, and in some cases, to men such as daytime talk-show host Phil Donohue, about their increasingly politicized personal decisions and debates. Not all women portrayed in pop culture were doing these things, of course—but both individual women and the media paid attention to the ones who were, because—like it or not—they were upending conventional notions of what women could and should do. In the 1980s, there were TV characters who seemed to be striving for feminist ideals, but for most of them—as it was for women in the real world—it was almost impossible to be feminist superwomen in a world that was still stubbornly unequal. There were Kate and Allie on the sitcom of the same name, two women who pooled their resources in the wake of divorce, raising their children together in what was both a clever housing arrangement and, more important, a necessary solution to working single motherhood. There were Murphy Brown and Molly Dodd, single working women grappling with having power in the professional sphere even as their single status was assumed to plague them. There was working-class mother and worker Roseanne, blithely snarking and cursing her way through the monotony of dead-ends jobs and ungrateful children on her titular sitcom. (Jennifer Reed's essay "Roseanne: A 'Killer Bitch' for Generation X" in the 1997 book *Third Wave Agenda: Being Feminist, Doing Feminism* proclaimed that Roseanne "voices the inevitable rage that comes when the knowledge created by feminist thinking and action encounters the intractability of oppressive forces.") At the movies, there were madcap comedies about women who stood up to discrimination in the workplace (*9 to 5*) and even more madcap takes on housewifery (*The Incredible Shrinking Woman, Freaky Friday*); there were princess narratives about hookers with hearts of gold (*Pretty Woman*) and cautionary tales about the perils of female sexual agency (*Fast Times at Ridgemont High*). And in music, there was MTV, which made a handful of women into rock stars while relegating countless others to a background in which they writhed, half-naked and faceless, for the better part of a decade.

The 1980s also saw female action heroes sidling up to their historically male counterparts; even if viewers didn't regard the onscreen ass-kicking undertaken by characters such as Ellen Ripley of the *Alien* series or Sarah Connor of the *Terminator* movies as putting feminist theory into practice, these characters were nevertheless expanding the definition of what women could do onscreen and validating individual women who longed to see other females doing more in the face of danger than looking pretty. For all of these women, feminism was a work in progress.

In the early 1990s, music was a primary site in which women were challenging the roles that the industry had constructed for them, and performers from Hole's Courtney Love to Meshell Ndegeocello to Fiona Apple were rattling the walls of music's girl ghettos and calling out the forces, both personal and institutional, that wanted to hold them back. And in the 2000s, pop culture is a stew of progressivism and backlash: On one TV network, a woman might be the president of the United States; on another, she's effusing that being a Pussycat Doll is the dream of a lifetime. *New York Times* columnist Maureen Dowd asserts that women want to be saved from their ambition, and the next day a righteous clutch of bloggers debate the point furiously. Feminism—that is, explicit references to the women's liberation movement—as reflected in popular culture might charitably be described as a funhouse-mirror view: You can discern the basic construction, but the overall effect is grotesquely distorted to maximize its worst features.

This is unsurprising when you consider that ever since there's been a women's movement, there have been public outcries against it. Simply put, everything about the women's movement has unsettled and dismayed people who are afraid of how the self-actualization and social and political equality of half the population will affect their own social and political power. And so myths about women and feminism were born at the same time as the women's movement itself, and they have proliferated and echoed throughout pop culture and news media like a game of Telephone, twisting and morphing into something many real women simply don't recognize. You've heard these myths before. Some of them are specifically about feminism, such as Pat Robertson's statement that "feminism encourages women to leave their husbands, kill their children, practice witchcraft, destroy capitalism, and become lesbians." Some are more generally about women and their changing desires and roles, such as the spate of news articles in the past decade that posit that because young girls are doing better in school, young boys' education and chances for success are compromised. Feminist mythmaking in the media counts as pop culture in itself. Take the "marriage and terrorists" statistic heard 'round the world in 1986: *Newsweek* magazine, in an article titled "Too Late for Prince Charming?", reported that single, college-educated women older than forty were more likely to die at the hands of terrorists than to marry. The statistic was greeted with skepticism by real, live women everywhere and at least one fictional woman: In the 1993 romantic comedy *Sleepless in Seattle*, Meg Ryan's character asserts that the figure couldn't be true. "It feels true," replies the coworker played by Rosie O'Donnell. In fact, Ryan's character's suspicions were correct—in a 2006 mea culpa, *Newsweek* admitted that the statistic was wrong, writing that, as of 1996—ten years after the original story—a single woman of forty in fact "had a 40.8 percent chance of eventually marrying," and it went on to note that her odds of marrying after forty these days "may be only slightly worse than the probability of correctly choosing 'heads' or 'tails' in a coin toss."

When pop culture presents feminism to the public via mainstream media, the results are mixed at best. For many women, this means that it's important to examine representations of women and agency in the expected places (network television, major labels), but it's even more important to start scouting the margins—the blogs, the underground publishing collectives, the tiny bedroom record labels—for alternatives and to begin creating them ourselves. Parsing feminism and pop culture is not as easy as looking vigilantly for what's "good" (that is, feminist) in pop culture and calling out what's "bad" (antifeminist and regressive).

Pop culture has always been about commerce, and feminism and pop culture will always be uneasy bedfellows in a larger culture that remains conflicted (to say the very least) about how much power, agency, and autonomy women should have. A significant chunk of the advertising industry has always been devoted to reaching women, and in most cases its messages have instructed women to be on guard, lest they compromise their most important quality: their looks. Lucky Strike magazine ads from as far back as 1928 touted the appetite-suppressing qualities of smoking; ones for Camay soap in that same decade warned women that "The Eyes of Men . . . The Eyes of Women Judge your Loveliness Every Day." (There's that darned male gaze again.) As the decades progressed, women were sold products to combat everything from halitosis and "intimate odor" to dry hair and naked toenails with copy that was about as subtle as a sharp stick in the eye. In her 1985 book, *Femininity*, Susan Brownmiller wrote of this state of affairs, "Because she is forced to concentrate on the minutiae of her bodily parts, a woman is never free of self-consciousness. She is never quite satisfied, and never secure, for desperate, unending absorption in the drive for perfect appearance—call it feminine vanity—is the ultimate restriction on freedom of mind."

The women's movement, however, gave advertising a new way to interact with women: namely, by speaking to them in the language of liberation. Advertisements still told women that their hair needed to be shinier and their bodies more toned for bikini season—they just did so more sneakily. From Virginia Slims' famous "You've come a long way, baby" campaign to "new woman" perfumes such as Charlie and Enjoli to Nike's "Just Do It" tagline in the 1980s and 1990s, corporations saw feminism as a fail-safe marketing tool and sought to link their products with images of strong, inspiring, and—of course—beautiful women. Advertising has increasingly capitalized on women's shifting status in society and culture, using riffs on feminist slogans and sly references to landmark liberations to sell everything from running shoes to diet frozen pizzas to diamond rings. But is it liberation or co-optation? And does one necessarily cancel out the other? If feminist ideology and discourse are simply plugged into existing models, and if the basic message—in this instance, the message to buy stuff—remains the same, is it feminism? Furthermore, when this advertising sits alongside contradictory content—as it might in a magazine such as *Teen Vogue*, in which articles on the dangers of eating disorders immediately precede fashion spreads peopled with rail-thin models—what message does that send? The very fact that pop culture depends on commerce for its reach and influence is what makes any association with feminism just a little bit suspect.

But Isn't Pop Culture Supposed to Be Fun?

An important point to make in any survey of women, feminism, and popular culture is that their intersections aren't simply ones of bloodless inquiry and pointed criticism. Popular culture is inescapable—it's all around us and getting more so every day. (If you want proof, try keeping a running tally, on a normal day in your life, of how many advertisements you see, how many websites you visit, how many TV shows, movies, or books you hear referenced in daily conversation, how many songs you hear snippets of in passing.) But pop culture is so powerful precisely because it can be so very engaging and pleasurable. What's better than going to a new action movie with friends after a long week of work, classes, or both? What's more satisfying than bouncing along to your new favorite song on your headphones? And I personally know many people (fine, I'm one of them) who look forward to a long plane ride for the sole reason that the time can be passed by digging into an issue of *Vanity Fair* or *Us Weekly*. Pop culture can be social, it can be secret, and it can be frivolous—but it can't be denied. The pleasure of consuming pop culture makes critiquing it one of the more challenging projects for feminists. Unlike eliminating the wage gap or securing reproductive autonomy for every woman, the relationship between feminism and pop culture has no finite, ultimate goal. There are many individual activists who use pop culture as a way to discuss women's rights—such as Jean Kilbourne, whose *Killing Us Softly* film series looks at images of women in advertising and its skewed lens on violence, love, and success, or Ani DiFranco, the independent singer-songwriter whose straightforward lyrics consistently address feminist issues. But there's no one success in the ongoing feminist project of critiquing and reforming pop culture that would cause women to high-five each other and say, "Yep, we're done here. All fixed."

What's Your Favorite Pop Culture Moment Ever?

"Sassy. Sigh. I remember being a tween and looking through my older sister's Seventeen and YM magazines and just not getting them. I thought the hope chest ads were hokey. I thought the fashions were lame. I wanted Seventeen's 'Sex and Your Body' column to be scandalous—or at least interesting—and was disappointed on every count. Then Sassy appeared, and I felt like it was talking to me. I got it. I saw myself in it. I devoured it monthly. I wrote my undergraduate senior thesis on it. I went to work there for almost a year as an unpaid intern. I got into teen magazines because of it, hoping to make changes from within. I care about feminism and pop culture because of it. I wrote a book for teen girls about decoding media messages and beauty ideals because of it. It shaped my identity, my career path, my critical-thinking skills, and my passions." —Audrey

"I'm always moved by movies about women and sports. My mother and I saw the movie A League of Their Own together, and I remember there was one scene where I started crying and I looked over at my mother and she was crying too. I can watch that movie and Bend It Like Beckham over and over. In both movies, the moments when the girls realize that they have this talent that's completely unrelated to expectations of them as women always ring true, and I love reaffirming that feeling in myself by watching them." —Donna

"A friend of mine in New York told me about this singer named Ani DiFranco and duped me a cassette tape of her first recording. It was just so raw and intense—it actually made me uncomfortable at first, but I started listening to it every single night on my headphones. It was the first time I had heard a girl use the word 'cunt'—there was a line in one of her songs that went 'My cunt is built like a wound that won't heal.' That was like, whoa. That line repeated in my head for days. It was just the most brave and honest thing I had ever heard in a song. It's insane when I think about it now, but I actually stopped seeing a guy because I played him the tape and he just shrugged and was like, 'It's okay, but her voice is annoying.' I haven't listened to Ani DiFranco in years, but that tape definitely made an impact." —Francesca

"My most profound moment was watching Thelma and Louise *with members of my college feminist collective (we were called Downer Feminist Council—terrible name) the summer in between my junior and senior years. We had this sense of great possibility and power that was connected to rage—like being pissed off was going to get me somewhere that felt really free. The next year, working at* Ms. *magazine, I fell for a woman who had a similar fixation on Callie Khouri's opus. I now see it as a particular moment in history—we were women nurtured on second wave feminist critiques of sexism, we were emerging from the fog of the backlash, we shrugged off those shackles and got wind of power and now what were we going to do? I think that film helped to usher in the sensibility of the third wave—*Thelma and Louise *go on their journey, raising their consciousness, but they don't get away. . . . We younger viewers started from their point of departure, and we didn't have to sacrifice ourselves to be free, or at least more free."* —Jennifer

"K.d. lang on the cover of Vanity Fair *magazine. That was hot. I realize now that it was some kind of lesbian fantasy aimed at guys—Cindy Crawford was giving k.d. a shave, in high heels and a bathing suit. But as a just-out lesbian, I really felt like, here is an icon who isn't ambiguous or closeted. I had it on my wall for a whole semester."* —Liz

"When I saw Girls Town *at a film festival with director Jim McKay in attendance, I was blown away by seeing a multiracial cast portray teenage girls in both a realistic and hopeful manner. I couldn't believe I was watching these strong characters bond with each other, critique racism and their treatment by men, and carry out retribution against rapists. Not only did they avoid death at the end of the film (unlike* Thelma and Louise*), they carried on with their lives with integrity and respect for each other. It was such a complicated and hopeful picture of teenage girls' lives and relationships. And it was directed by a white man who was smart enough to realize he couldn't do justice to the story without women's input; the young women in the film helped write it and improvised much of their own dialogue. It gave the film its realistic feel and showed how powerful collaborative feminist projects involving all genders can be."* —Wendy

So what could a feminist reclamation of—or just an improvement on—pop culture look like? Well, let's start with Hollywood: With more feminist directors, producers, screenwriters, and network heads, perhaps women would stop being relegated to wife-and-girlfriend roles in action movies. Perhaps parts created for women of color would be not only more plentiful but also less stereotypical. Perhaps the juiciest roles for women—the ones that garner them attention, accolades, and little gold men—would be something other than, as Shirley MacLaine famously put it, "hookers, victims, and doormats." That time, as of today, seems far off: In the fall of 2007, film-industry columnist Nikki Finke leaked an internal studio missive from Warner Bros.' president of production, Jeff Robinov, announcing that the studio would no longer be making films with female leads. In a less-than-robust rebuttal, the studio issued a statement via the industry magazine *Variety*: "Contrary to recent reports in the blogosphere, Warner Bros. is still committed to women."

Then there's television. It's a little too simple to say that in a more feminist pop culture, we wouldn't see women in bikinis competing with each other to win a diamond ring from a man they've known for ten minutes, or looping around stripper poles on nearly every cable channel, or wearing tiny matching dresses and smiling toothy, Vaselined smiles while holding briefcases full of money. But it's certain that we wouldn't see quite so many of them.

What else would look different? Well, female musicians wouldn't be encouraged to sex up their images for major-label deals or coverage in music magazines or on MTV. Female comedians would have as many sitcom deals as their male counterparts, and if some yahoo sent up the inevitable cry of "But women aren't funny!" there'd be a plethora of people ready to prove him wrong. The term "chick lit" wouldn't exist to describe/denigrate books written by women that happen to be about relationships.

Some people used to think that having more women in positions of power at publishing houses, movie studios, record companies, and TV networks would make a difference. Yet even when women have held these positions of influence, their companies still produce plenty of material that demeans, objectifies, and insults women. Case in point: Sheila Nevins, as the president of HBO's documentary and family programming, produced many incredible, award-winning documentaries, but she's also responsible for the channel's recent obsession with glamorizing sex work, executive-producing HBO's series about strippers (*G-String Divas*), about porn stars (*Pornucopia: Going Down in the Valley*), and about prostitutes (*Cathouse; Cathouse 2: Back in the Saddle*). There's simply no mandate that a woman, by virtue of being in power, will make choices that will elevate all women or that other women will automatically approve of. Getting one or two seats for women at the proverbial table won't guarantee that the face of pop culture becomes one that's friendlier to women; it's simply one part of a larger push for women to be more proactive, more unapologetic, and more determined to make spaces in pop culture that represent all the dimensions of women's lives. But in the meantime, there's nothing wrong with loving, consuming, and creating pop culture with an eye toward how it can be better: smarter, less insulting to women (and men, for that matter), more diverse, and less hell-bent on perpetuating ugly and unhelpful stereotypes. And understanding more about feminism and pop culture's long, difficult, and occasionally fruitful relationship is a good way to start.

AMERICAN DREAMS, STIFLED REALITIES: WOMEN AND POP CULTURE IN THE 1940S, '50S, AND '60S

THE BIRTH OF WHAT WE think of as modern popular culture—the white-noise buzz of TV and radio and film and advertising—happened in the early 1940s and coincided with World War II. There was new technology; the television made its popular debut in 1942. There was a national sense of community fostered by the war; patriotic posters and advertisements offered a romanticized picture of a triumphing America, and fatherly voices came over the airwaves each night with news and dispatches from the front. There was a new economic prosperity, thanks to the war-related commerce that had pulled the United States out of the Depression of the 1930s. Finally, there were media that were finding ever-new ways to market to potential audiences, with programming and advertising that appealed to as many people as possible in one stroke—the oft-invoked "lowest common denominator."

For women, popular culture has always been a sinister mix of friend and foe—a "frenemy," if you will. It draws us in with pretty images, sweet sounds, and arresting promises—and it's only upon looking more closely that we realize what it's really trying to tell us and sell us. Even the best movies, the giddiest television romps, the most memorable ad campaigns speak of what women can and should—or shouldn't—be. And to look back to the first half of the twentieth century is to realize that its varied pop culture—from an ad for diapers to a smoky film noir—had one thing in common: a picture of women's lives that was fraught with contradictions, questions, and deeply mixed messages.

Consuming Passions: Women in Advertising

Advertising has always had one chief aim: to make a consumer want to buy a product by any means necessary. And to advertise to women, this has meant that female consumers are made to feel insecure and off balance for most of their waking moments: too short, too tall, too fat, too skinny, dull-haired, lumpy-bottomed, flat-chested, thin-lipped, too pale, not pale enough, too smart, too dumb, not sexy, a lax housekeeper, a lazy cook, a bad mother, a neglectful spouse. In each of these indictments of women's appearance or temperament, there's a product to be sold, whether it's mascara or furniture polish or children's cold medicine. And in its bids for consumers, advertising has been a consistent standard-bearer of how our society sees the role of women.

Beginning in the late 1800s, women played two discrete roles in advertising. In ads aimed at men, women appeared as sexy pinups alongside manly products, their skirts accidentally blown up by armored tubing or hooked onto fishing poles. Male-only work environments were the targets of promotional calendars featuring scantily clad lovelies in provocative poses. Though the pinups distributed to, say, a machine shop by a parts manufacturer might have nothing to do with that industry, they were an easy way to make sure that the men in the shop associated that manufacturer with the smiling, bare-breasted girls on that calendar. A few men made painting pinups into an art form: Alberto Vargas and George Petty, for instance, would both become famous for their calendars and *Esquire* magazine pinups, which featured bodacious, come-hither women who looked naked no matter what they wore.

Ads aimed at women, however, were much more about romance than about sex. Advertisers pitched their female audiences with the language of love: "adoration," "glamour," "loveliness," and "femininity" were oft-used catchwords in ad copy, ascribing these qualities to women who used products varying from Lux dishwashing soap flakes to Lucky Strike cigarettes. Such ads exhorted women to "Keep that schoolgirl complexion," "Be the girl he marries . . . forever," and "Bring out those romantic curves that will make your bust line your beauty line." Meanwhile, ads that warned women of dry skin or "intimate" odors used the flip side of romance—cursed loneliness—to make their pitches heard. "Often a bridesmaid but never a bride," tsked one 1920s-era Listerine ad, which went on to tell the tragic story of Edna: "Edna's case was really a pathetic one. Like every woman, her primary ambition was to marry. Most of the girls of her set were married—or about to be. Yet not one possessed more grace or charm or loveliness than she. And as her birthdays crept gradually toward that thirty-mark, marriage seemed farther from her life than ever."

The reason for Miss Edna's sad state? Halitosis, folks. If only Edna knew about Listerine, the ads mourned, she might still marry (and thus, was the subtext, give her life some purpose). A similarly classic ad was for Lysol, which we now know as a powerful room deodorizer but which, back in the day, was recommended for an entirely different kind of deodorizing. A 1948 ad for the product pictured a woman wringing her hands as her husband exited the room; the question "Why does she spend the evenings alone?" boomed below. The answer? "Wives often lose the precious air of romance, doctors say, for lack of the intimate daintiness dependent on effective douching. For this, look to reliable 'Lysol' brand disinfectant."

And when ads weren't reminding women that their happiness depended on keeping dainty and covering or suppressing their naturally hideous odors, they had plenty to say about women's roles as wives and mothers. A 1947 ad for Johnson's Baby Oil and Baby Powder featured a giant baby walking his tiny mother on a leash, with copy that read, "Whoa, Mom! Can't you take it?" The ad used a conversation between the enormous tyke and his diminutive caregiver to point out that, by not rubbing and sprinkling her son with Johnson & Johnson products, this mother was dangerously lax. "I haven't been a careful mother, have I? Watch me *reform*!" promises the mother by ad's end. A 1942 Nabisco ad titled "How one Mother met her family's most troublesome 'health problem'" described a woman whose husband, son, and father were plagued by constipation. After this mother introduced the company's 100% Bran cereal into their diets, however, all was well. Though the idea that women alone were responsible for mothering not only their children but their husbands as well seems awfully retro to us now, at the time ads such as these weren't meant to reflect women's weakness but rather their power.

It almost goes without saying that the women in all of these ads were white and middle class. Until the 1960s, and in many cases even later, the only black female images to be found in ads in mainstream magazines (and, later, on television) were those of pancake mascot Aunt Jemima; representations of Latina and Asian women, to say nothing of other ethnicities such as Greek or Jewish, were entirely absent. It was these white, blank-slate women—who didn't earn all or even part of their families' income, but who were responsible for the household purchasing—whose eyes and wallets advertisers sought to capture. It wasn't feminism, exactly, but the linking of purchasing power with social power would become an ever-more-persistent thread in pop culture aimed at women. *Ladies' Home Journal* even adopted the phrase "Never underestimate the power of a woman" as its slogan—though the power the magazine espoused had mostly to do with choosing the best cold remedies and cuts of meat.

Though advertisements for creams, soaps, and undergarments had been part of women's pop culture since the nineteenth century, the biggest sales pitch to women didn't come about until World War II—and it wasn't for a product but was instead for an entirely new role women could play. As men left their jobs to go fight the war, women were suddenly the target of a very different kind of advertising, one that urged them to stop worrying about their complexions and worry instead about their country.

In decades past, and particularly during the Great Depression in the 1930s, women who could afford not to work outside the home—again, largely white and middle-class women—were urged not to. The logic was that every woman who entered the workforce was taking a job away from a man. (Twenty-six states even had laws stating that married women could not be employed.) But with men leaving the American workforce in droves, women were suddenly being told that it was their patriotic duty to get out into the shops and the factories and keep their country's economy moving. The U.S. Office of War Information teamed up with women's magazines and radio and movie producers to create ads and newsreels in which sassy, smiling women in kerchiefs and work shirts were America's sweethearts, dutifully filling the men's shoes but never losing their femininity in the process.

The effort to move middle-class women into the workforce demanded that the United States acknowledge, at least to some extent, its own hypocrisy and sexism. As Maria Elena Buszek points out in *Pin-up Grrrls: Feminism, Sexuality, Popular Culture:* "President Franklin D. Roosevelt's 1942 Columbus Day speech directly addressed the fact that traditional biases would not be tolerated in the wartime workforce: 'In some communities employers dislike to hire women. In others they are reluctant to hire Negroes. We can no longer afford to indulge such prejudice.' As a result, women and people of color on the home front were soon asked to learn to perform roles that years, even months earlier had been deemed beyond their physical and intellectual capabilities."

More than six million women answered the call of duty, thanks in part to the propaganda efforts that flattered women by positioning them as central to their country's success in the war. The OWI produced posters suggesting that the female war worker—rather than Hollywood starlets or *Esquire* centerfolds—was the soldier's "real pin-up girl"; posters recruiting women for jobs in the military featured illustrations of uniformed women as aspirational as those in any complexion-soap ad. No longer valued only as wives and mothers, women were suddenly positioned as both the reason men should keep fighting the war and the fuel behind their country's efforts to do so.

World War II and the years immediately following it, in fact, were a time when the images of women in advertising literally dictated to them their roles in society. They were supposed to be interim heads

For your country's sake today-

For your own sake tomorrow

GO TO THE NEAREST RECRUITING STATION
OF THE ARMED SERVICE OF YOUR CHOICE

© The National Archives

World War II recruiting posters positioned women as central to the war effort.

of households, of course, as instructed by the myriad pitches in women's magazines that showed mothers and children donating tin cans and toothpaste tubes to the war effort and cooking ingenious dinners with their rationed foodstuffs. They were supposed to be glamourpusses whose bountiful charms and willing kisses were sent, in the form of pinups, to the soldiers abroad as promises of what awaited them back at home. And they were supposed to be sassy, spunky pinch hitters in the workforce, according to that iconic Rosie the Riveter image that beckoned from OWI posters.

But these images changed once the war was over and the boys came home. The media forces that had hurried women into the factories were now herding them back into the home to make room for men—for whom, it was understood, the workforce was their rightful place. Women were no longer wooed with images of themselves as competent welders or military nurses; instead, the postwar era of advertising ushered in a new set of representations of women as either dutiful wives and mothers or childlike sex kittens.

Sacrificing Mothers and Femmes Fatales: Women on Screen

In Hollywood, women fared somewhat differently, if not much better. Much like many people wring their hands today over declining standards of decency in film and television, during the 1920s Hollywood's booming film industry was accused of promoting everything from prostitution to gambling to atheism. A flashpoint for these claims occurred in 1921, when actor "Fatty" Arbuckle was accused of raping a young actress with a wine bottle; the young woman died of internal injuries, and in the midst of the sensational manslaughter trial that followed, the country buzzed with talk of the film industry's lawless, immoral influence on impressionable minds. Since the Supreme Court had ruled in 1915 that motion pictures were not covered under the First Amendment's freedom-of-speech protections, Hollywood studios feared that government censorship couldn't be far off. They decided that self-regulation was better than federal regulation, and the Motion Picture Production Code of 1930, now known as the Hays Code, was born. The Hays Code set out moral guidelines for film plots and representations, placing limits on the violence, sexuality, nudity, and "moral conduct" that could be shown onscreen. In laying out the code, its authors wrote: "Mankind has always recognized the importance of entertainment and its value in rebuilding the bodies and souls of human beings. But it has always recognized that entertainment can be a character either HELPFUL or HARMFUL to the human race, and in consequence has clearly distinguished between: a. Entertainment which tends to improve the race, or at least to re-create and rebuild human beings exhausted with the realities of life; and b. Entertainment which tends to degrade human beings, or to lower their standards of life and living."

The Hays Code was designed to dispense with any films that wallowed in degrading, standard-lowering behavior. Under the code, screen kisses were brief; blaspheming was a no-no; violence and crime happened in shadows; even belly buttons were deemed vulgar. Nudity and sexually suggestive movements were prohibited, as were depictions of homosexuality, interracial romance, or other so-called sex perversions. And though adultery and pre- or extramarital sex were acknowledged by the code to be occasionally necessary plot points, filmmakers were to avoid presenting them as anything other than immoral.

The Hays Code was enforced from 1934 until 1968 and had a profound effect on the way women were depicted in motion pictures during those years. Before the Hays Code was adopted, women's roles in film were not only racier but more realistic. Take the subject of divorce: Pre–Hays Code, a number of Hollywood films dealt with the subject in what would seem by current standards to be both candid and daring. One of the most well known of these was 1930s *The Divorcee*, starring Norma Shearer. In the film, she plays a woman whose husband has an affair with another woman; when Shearer's character finds out, the husband pleads with her to understand that the infidelity meant nothing. Instead of forgiving him, she has an affair herself—a tit-for-tat move that leads to her husband's walking out. The movie was a ferocious attack on the double standard of sexual behavior, and it earned Shearer an Academy Award—but had it been made just five years later, its plotline might never have been approved, since the Hays Code demanded that the sanctity of marriage be upheld onscreen, with divorce employed only as a last resort.

Then there was the subject of women's onscreen sexual agency. In a number of pre-code films, female leads were shamelessly sassy and questionably moral and were memorably essayed by Jean Harlow, Clara Bow, Mae West, Myrna Loy, and Marlene Dietrich, among others. In *Red-Headed Woman*, for instance, Harlow played the title character, a brazen social climber who used her sexual charms to seduce a series of willing men, starting with her boss and moving on to a wealthy businessman; in *The Blue Angel*, Dietrich defined the role of the vixen in her portrayal of a gentleman's-club headliner who unwittingly becomes the downfall of one of her hapless admirers.

Elsewhere, pre-code women on screen held powerful jobs, had affairs with married men, birthed babies out of wedlock, and seduced other women—and those were the comedies! But these socially and sexually empowered women are often forgotten when we talk about movies in "the old days," because once the Hays Code was enforced, it became difficult to find such women in the theaters. Lesbian themes, once overt in such films as *Mädchen in Uniform* and *Queen Christina*, were completely quashed: Though movie producer Samuel Goldwyn bought the film rights to Lillian Hellman's lesbian-themed drama *The Children's Hour*, the homosexual content of the play was nowhere to be seen in his 1936 film version, titled *These Three*. (The film was remade in 1961 as a much more faithful adaptation starring Audrey Hepburn and Shirley MacLaine.) And the swaggering heterosexual pleasure and agency ascribed to starlets such as Harlow and Loy went away when the code's moral hammer dropped. "The Code came to prevent women from having fun," wrote Mick LaSalle in his book *Complicated Women: Sex and Power in Pre-Code Hollywood*. "It was designed to put the genie back in the bottle—and the wife back in the kitchen."

The results of the Hays Code weren't quite so simple, but characterizations of women in post-code films were indeed less brazen, less sexual, and far less powerful. The new female figure in film was one who was somehow imperiled—by love, by sickness, or by circumstance—and it was around this figure that a new genre of film called "the woman's picture" revolved. Such movies, which were popular in the 1930s, '40s, and '50s, responded to Hays Code regulations by scripting a heavy-handed moralism into dramas about women victimized by life. Women's pictures were directed mostly by men—notable purveyors included Douglas Sirk, George Cukor, and William Wyler—but focused squarely on female leads. They tended toward melodrama—what film critic Molly Haskell, in *From Reverence to Rape: The Treatment of Women in the Movies*, called "soft-core emotional porn for the frustrated housewife"— with themes of sacrifice (either maternal or romantic) and suffering (either romantic or physical) foremost in their plots. The suffering category boasted such multihanky weepers as *Dark Victory*, which starred Bette Davis as a young society woman diagnosed with a brain tumor who falls in love with her doctor. But the films that still stand as classics of the woman's-film era are the ones in the sacrifice category that tell the story of a woman whose greatest life choices are driven by mother love.

The uncontested queen of the maternal-sacrifice movies is *Stella*

Girls in the 'Wood: Racism on and off the silver screen

The first African American woman to be nominated for an Academy Award couldn't even attend the premiere of her own movie in Atlanta, Georgia. The actress was Hattie McDaniel, the film was 1939's *Gone with the Wind*, and the atmosphere in both the United States and Hollywood was one of unabashed racism. McDaniel won the Best Supporting Actress Oscar for her role as Mammy, Scarlett O'Hara's long-suffering maid, but her night of glory did little to change the status of women of color in a film industry that was plagued by deeply ingrained institutional racism.

McDaniel started her career in radio as "Hi-Hat Hattie," a nosy maid character on a radio serial called *The Optimistic Do-Nut Hour*; unlike white radio performers, she was paid so little that she worked as a maid in real life as well. Upon breaking into film, she became one of a clutch of black actresses, along with Louise Beavers and Ethel Waters, whose rise to fame was predicated on playing maids, mammies, and slaves. Though she famously remarked that "I'd rather play a maid and make $700 a week than be one for $7," McDaniel and her black contemporaries in film were consistent targets of criticism from groups such as the NAACP, which felt that black actors were only perpetuating stereotypes of African Americans by accepting roles that had them bowing and scraping to white characters.

But for actors of color in Hollywood, there was little choice but to either take the roles that were available or not work at all. Another actress who

Dallas, first made in the silent era as an adaptation of the novel by Olive Higgins Prouty and remade in 1937. The 1937 version featured Barbara Stanwyck as Stella, a working-class girl who marries a man of high-society breeding, if not high-society fortune, who can never quite accept her as she is. They divorce, and he goes on to marry an old flame, leaving Stella stung and determined to make sure their daughter, Laurel, has all the social advantages she needs to fit into her father's new life—even if it means that she herself has to stay out of it. Stella is a complicated character, both relatable and embarrassing, and her struggled with these limitations was Anna May Wong, the Chinese American daughter of an immigrant laundryman, who Americanized her given name, Wong Liu Tsong, and broke into the movie industry with memorable "exotic" roles such as Tiger Lily in 1924's *Peter Pan* and Lotus Flower in 1922's *The Toll of the Sea*, an update of the classic opera *Madame Butterfly*. Though irrefutably a leading lady in both looks and talent, Wong's career was severely limited by Hollywood racism. For one thing, actors of color—men and women alike—were paid far less for their work than their white counterparts. And despite the success of Mexican actresses Lupe Velez and Dolores del Rio in films of the 1920s and '30s, the Hays Code inscribed overt racism into the film industry with anti-miscegenation laws that prohibited actors of different races from performing romantic scenes together. And a leading lady without a love story wasn't exactly a hot property in Hollywood.

As Hollywood has aged, so have its strictures: Dorothy Dandridge suffered from them in the 1950s, despite being the first African American actress to be nominated for a Best Actress Oscar; Cicely Tyson, Ruby Dee, Lena Horne, Whoopi Goldberg, and Halle Berry have followed in her celebrated tracks, famous in their own right but still faced with a narrow range of available roles. Asian and Latina actresses have fared not much better, with only a handful cast in leading roles—and even then, their roles are often limited by the industry's persistent urge to exoticize nonwhite women. And though anti-miscegenation laws seem as outdated to us now as separate drinking fountains for blacks and whites, it's rare to see an interracial pairing on movie screens—just another reminder of Hollywood's imperfect reflections of real women and real life.

ultimate act of sacrifice—walking out of her daughter's life—is meant to be simultaneously heartbreaking and maddening.

Other classics of maternal sacrifice include *Imitation of Life*, made in 1934 and again in 1959, *Madame X* (so good it was remade three times), *All That Heaven Allows*, and *Mildred Pierce*, all of which featured women who, for one reason or another, are done wrong by their ungrateful children, yet who bravely soldier on as dutiful mothers. *Mildred Pierce*, in particular, is considered a parable of post–World War II anxiety about women as workplace threats to men. In the 1945 film, Joan Crawford plays the title character, a woman who builds a financially successful restaurant business but in the process neglects the emotional work of motherhood. Her daughter, Veda, goes from brattiness to immorality to, eventually, murder. And it all could have been avoided, the film implies, if only Mildred hadn't been so independent, so powerful, and so successful.

Haskell notes of these films: "Because the woman's film was designed for and tailored to a certain market, its recurrent themes represent the closest things to an expression of the collective drives, conscious and unconscious, of American women, of their avowed obligations and their unconscious resistance." And, indeed, the subtext of these films can best be summed up as "You can't have it all—and if you're uppity enough to think you can, you'll be punished for it." In women's pictures, the protagonists find love, but they have to lose their children for it. They're financially successful, but their children resent them and end up as murderers. They have wonderful lives, but they die young of brain tumors. The themes of these films have gone on to reverberate throughout Hollywood—in fact, they echo throughout pop culture in general. Women are punished for being martyrs but punished too when they refuse to be.

The flip side of the 1940s woman's film was the film noir, and many of the same actresses who sacrificed everything for their partners and children got their symbolic payback in movies of this genre. As vamps, liars, criminals, and double-crossers, film noir's women were both beautiful and treacherous, and they embodied everything that a woman's-film heroine was supposed to suppress—and because they almost always got their comeuppance, they fit neatly in line with Hays Code standards of morality. Barbara Stanwyck in *Double Indemnity*, Jane Greer in *Out of the Past*, Veronica Lake in *This Gun for Hire*, and Lauren Bacall in *The Big Sleep*, among many others, were sultry, mysterious women who infiltrated the shadowy world of men for even shadier purposes. Their power was sexual, of course, but it was also intellectual—and it was their brains that were meant to come across on screen as the bigger threat. These weren't just women; these were *dames*.

Dames didn't starch your shirts and admire your biceps; they got you to kill for them and then turned you in to the cops.

But though film-noir heroines can today be seen through a retro lens as proto-feminist characters, it's not quite that simple. In these films, the banter and chemistry between the male and female leads is based not so much on equality between them as it is on mutual distrust and fear. No wonder: In *Gaslight*, a husband isolates his wife and tricks her into believing she's going mad in order to cover up his own murderous past; *Out of the Past*'s central couple dies in a mutual double-cross, and in the extremely convoluted *The Big Sleep*, nobody is exempt from suspicion. As Haskell points out about these film-noir couplings, "Where once sexual antagonism was a game, a pretext, a holding action until the underlying affinity could emerge, attraction is now the illusion, the decoy, the duplicitous façade." In other words, even when men's and women's roles weren't rigidly defined as pursuer/pursued or bad seed/good soul, they were portrayed as being on opposite sides of a vast chasm. The idea of relationships as a "battle of the sexes" didn't begin with film noir, of course, but in the genre it found one of its most literal depictions in popular culture.

The Curse of the Happy Housewife: Women on TV

And then there was TV, which in many ways came to be more synonymous with pop culture than any other medium. Families gathered 'round it to watch the news and eat dinner on TV trays; later, "TV dinners" made it even easier for families to combine their together time with TV time. Television responded with a slew of shows about family itself.

Perhaps more than any other pop culture product, the sitcoms produced from the mid-1940s to the early 1960s are responsible for how Americans think about the role of women in that era. These shows did not reflect the reality of every woman—as with advertising and movies, they focused almost exclusively on the lives of white, middle-class women. From *The Honeymooners* and *I Love Lucy* to *Father Knows Best* and *The Donna Reed Show*, viewers learned that the role of women—whether they were as loudmouthed as Lucy or as demure as Donna—was to hold down the home front, raise the kiddies, and get the meat loaf on the table when Dad got home from work. The humor in these shows was derived, in fact, from these very expectations. When Honeymooner Ralph Kramden issued his exasperated threats to send wife Alice "to the moon!" for some small domestic infraction, or when Lucy smuggled a bunch of cheese onto an airplane in the form of a swaddled baby, viewers could laugh without feeling uncomfortable that the status quo had been messed with.

But unlike the woman's pictures of the 1940s and '50s, in which women were the axis around which the story revolved, women on TV in this era were more often than not relegated to the sidelines. Perhaps as part of a postwar effort to assure men's authority, husbands and fathers were made the linchpins of these shows, judging and scolding their wives and providing the moral fiber of family life. Lucy's wild schemes, for instance, were so cringeworthy in part because the audience knew they would get her in trouble with Ricky; Wally and the Beav on *Leave It to Beaver* were scolded by both parents for their pranks, but it was their father's understanding and forgiveness that made it all better. And *Father Knows Best?* Well, it's right there in the title.

And yet, even within women's narrow roles on television, there were flashes of the domestic resistance that would more fully rear its head in the coming decades. In *Where the Girls Are: Growing Up Female with the Mass Media*, Susan J. Douglas describes "transgressive" characters such as Lucy and Alice as well as *Your Show of Shows'* Imogene Coca and Gracie Allen of *The Burns and Allen Show*. Of Ball and Coca, she writes, "These women and their bodies refused to be contained in the home or limited by the prevailing orthodoxy about appropriate female comportment. Their voices mattered too; often they were loud, they weren't afraid to yell, and they didn't back away from verbal combat."

But from a mass viewpoint, the defining characteristic of the sitcom housewife of the 1950s was perfection, either real or hoped-for. Her kitchen floors gleamed, her children's noses never ran, and she herself was trim and lipsticked from morning 'til night. Current events, no.

Social events, yes. This pursuit of perfection was not, in fact, the reality of all women, many of whom had joined the workforce. In 1955, more American women held jobs outside the home than at any other time up to that point; by 1960, 40 percent of women (including white, middle-class mothers) worked outside the home. And, contrary to what happy-family propaganda put forth, divorce rates spiked twice after World War II—once at the end of the war and again in the mid-1950s. But no pop culture centered on the women described by those statistics.

In the television series I Love Lucy, *Lucille Ball played the loudmouthed title character whose crazy schemes often met with reproach from her husband, Ricky.*

© CBS Television and Desilu, too, LLC

The image of the happy 1950s homemaker was one that became indelible through hindsight. There were several TV shows of the 1950s that focused on working-class families, both white and black, in which the women of the house had more pressing concerns than ring around the collar. There was the Jewish Molly Goldberg of tenement-house comedy *The Goldbergs* (which ran from 1952 to 1956), Norwegian immigrant Marta Hansen on *Mama* (1949–1956), and the titular black heroine of *Beulah* (1950–1953). Each of these shows built up a faithful following in their early incarnations as either radio shows (*The Goldbergs* and *Beulah*) or stage plays (*Mama* was based on the much-loved drama *I Remember Mama*). All were warm, gently comedic stories of working-class people struggling with both everyday family dramas and the challenges of cultural assimilation (or, in the case of *Beulah*, struggling against charges that the main character was little more than a live-action Aunt Jemima). But when social conservatives and hand-wringing politicians preaching on moral decline trot out the image of the 1950s-era middle-class family—Mom, Dad, Dick, and Jane—as the paragon to which Americans should aspire to return, they're not talking about *The Goldbergs*. As Stephanie Coontz points out in her 1992 book *The Way We Never Were: America's Families and the Nostalgia Trap*, what these moral gatekeepers don't get is that the male-breadwinning, female-submissive, green-bean-casserole-and-ambrosia-salad *Leave It to Beaver* model never existed in the form we're most nostalgic for.

> *Like most visions of a "golden age," the "traditional family" my students describe evaporates on closer examination. It is an ahistorial amalgam of structures, values, and behaviors that never coexisted in the same time and place. The notion that traditional families fostered intense intimacy between husbands and wives while creating mothers who were totally available to their children, for example, is an idea that combines some characteristics of the white, middle-class family in the mid-nineteenth century and some of a rival family ideal first articulated in the 1920s. . . . The hybrid idea that a woman can be fully absorbed with her youngsters while simultaneously maintaining passionate sexual excitement with her husband was a 1950s invention that drove thousands of women to therapists, tranquilizers, and alcohol when they actually tried to live up to it.*

And yet, that nostalgia sells. Coontz's students very likely got their ideas about the nuclear family from classic sitcoms that have been rebroadcast for years on television. In the mid- to late 1980s, cable channel Nickelodeon began its "Nick at Nite" programming, which reran classic sitcoms such as *Leave It to Beaver*, *Dennis the Menace*, *The Patty Duke Show*, and more. What was no doubt meant as a winking look back kicked off a torrent of wistfulness for these "golden years" as seen through the TV camera. But later TV shows and movies drew back a curtain to reveal the folly of such nostalgia, particularly with regard to women's roles. In the 1998 film *Pleasantville*, for instance, the mother in a revered *Father Knows Best*–type TV series shows severe cracks in her facade of wifely perfection, finding happiness only after she rebels against her literally colorless existence and has an affair with the owner of a local diner. And in the 2003 film *Mona Lisa Smile*, set in 1953 at Wellesley College, a married coed who initially delights in the trappings of housewifery—in one scene, she reveals her new washer and dryer like an excited game-show hostess—is shocked when she discovers that the reality of daily life as homemaker isn't all she was led to believe it would be.

To say that the popular culture of the two decades after World War II sent mixed messages to women would be a massive understatement. On the one hand, women were told that their natural realm was the kitchen and the nursery; on the other, characters such as Lucy and Gracie proved every day that women were well aware of the roles they played as wives and mothers, and we laughed at how they subverted those roles. *Ladies' Home Journal* ran a monthly column, "If You Ask Me," in which former first lady and lifelong political progressive Eleanor Roosevelt opined on women's rights and issued statements such as, "I think girls should have the same opportunities as boys"; the same magazine, however, regularly dissuaded women from disagreeing with or challenging their husbands, and it put the onus of a family's happiness squarely on the shoulders of women and their ability to cook, clean, mother, mediate, and prettify the lives of those around them. There weren't yet words to describe this contradictory phenomenon in the 1950s and early 1960s, but there soon would be.

Rebelling, in Music, and in Real Life

By the late 1960s, American audiences had become used to male rebellion as a recurring theme in both real-life adolescence and popular culture. Books such as *The Catcher in the Rye* and *On the Road* and movies such as *Rebel Without a Cause*, *The Graduate*, and *To Sir, with*

Bottled Up: How TV Curbed Female Power

In the perky, fluffy world of pre-second wave popular culture, the idea that girls and women might rebel against painstakingly prescribed gender roles must have been awfully frightening. At least, that seems to be the best explanation for the increasingly outrageous premises of television comedies of the 1960s and '70s, wherein women appeared as witches and genies whose unpredictable powers served as way-too-obvious metaphors for womanly rebellion.

Take *Bewitched*, which gave us Samantha Andrews, a housewife with magical powers, and her drip of a husband, Darrin, who constantly begged her not to use them. From the start, the show's comedy lay in the fact that though Samantha was the perfect wife—beautiful, charming, socially graceful—she just couldn't help using her benign witchcraft to meddle in the lives of others, especially Darrin. To complicate matters, both her mother and her daughter were also witches, a state of affairs that made Darrin both a source of pity—all those pesky women!—and a reflection of a growing real-life male anxiety about the ways modern women might overshadow and make useless the men in their lives.

Bewitched wasn't supposed to make people ponder the issues of masculine supremacy and female submission, of course—it was a goofy, fun little show and a huge hit, running on ABC from 1964 to 1972. But many feminists have seen in *Bewitched* a parable of early second wave feminism, and in Samantha an embodiment of the way women might enact everyday rebellion from behind the facade of the perfect housewife. And

Love served up a tacit awareness of male angst. Audiences understood that there could be brief periods of turmoil in a young man's life without ruining the rest of it. At the end of *The Graduate*, when Benjamin Braddock busts up the wedding of his crush—who just happens to be the daughter of his lover, Mrs. Robinson—and they run off together, we don't know exactly what's going to happen to him. But the ending is purposely, hopefully vague, and we can reasonably expect him to grow eventually into an upstanding, run-of-the-mill husband and father with no more than a wistful glance backward.

because Samantha didn't use her magical powers only to clean sinkloads of dishes in an instant or to ensure that Darrin advanced at his job—she also used them for a greater good—she offered proof (fantastical though it was) that women might have an effect on the public sphere, not just on their own realm.

Then there was Jeannie, whose powers were literally bottled up by her male caretaker on *I Dream of Jeannie*. The sitcom, which ran for five seasons starting in 1964, told the story of astronaut Tony Nelson and the two-thousand-year-old genie he discovers on a deserted island. Once he sets her free—temporarily, of course—the well-preserved, scantily clad Jeannie is indebted to her "master" and accompanies him back to civilian life. Hijinks ensue, naturally, since Jeannie is ill equipped for modern life and, in her earnestness to serve Major Nelson—and her jealousy of others in his life—ends up being more trouble than he bargained for. And, much like Samantha's in *Bewitched*, her magical powers have to be kept under control lest they make a fool out of the man in her life.

Taken together, *Bewitched* and *Jeannie* were a surreal dyad of anxiety about female rebellion against gender roles. They embodied the contradictions facing real women at the time, both offering a winking facet of wish fulfillment (what housewife wouldn't want to take care of the housework merely by wiggling her nose?) and a warning of what might happen to a woman whose feminine power can be uncorked at will. With a knowing wink, they hinted at the push toward female emancipation that was to come while simultaneously affirming the conventional wisdom that women were most fulfilled when they were assisting their male partners and assuring their success.

Rebellion for girls and women was a little different—and from a societal perspective, wholly frightening. A boys-will-be-boys mentality has always excused the youthful rebellions and transgressions of boys; girls' experimentations, though, had lasting consequences. Contrast *The Graduate*, for instance, with the 1961 movie *Splendor in the Grass*, in which Natalie Wood played Deanie, a teen who becomes so addled by her kept-in-check sexual desire that she literally can't function and ends up in a sanatorium. The movie posited rebellion for girls as a double-edged sword—you could give in to your rebellious desire to not be a "good girl"—as the sister of the movie's hero, Bud, does—and disgrace your family and ruin your reputation, or you could follow the rules and still be punished with madness, like poor doomed Deanie.

So this was the bind in which the pre–second wave teen girl found herself: She wanted freedom and chafed against rigid girl-world roles, yet she also still wanted the traditional rewards of femininity—love, admiration, validation by family and peers. This was a concept expressed not just on TV shows such as *Bewitched*, *Gidget*, and *I Dream of Jeannie*, but in many pockets of popular culture. And the contradiction was expressed perhaps most eloquently in the pop music of the 1960s by musicians and girl groups who made both the indignities and the joys of femalehood central to their sound.

They sang as if they were born to do so, but the formation of girl groups such as the Shirelles, the Exciters, the Shangri-Las, and the Ronettes was actually a calculated move by music producers and promoters to find a new, modern audience. Pop music was an industry always looking for a new hit-making formula, and the young, often black and poor teens who came to be girl groups were, at the end of the day, merely product. For the most part, girl groups were the creations of men—men discovered and molded them, were involved in writing and producing their songs, and selected their "look." But what the songs of these groups offered to pop culture was a window into the hidden emotional life of girls, as trivial as it often seemed: Both confident and confused, sexual and scared, the tunes they sang gave a new dimension to pop culture and were pitched directly at a female audience.

The twin centers of the girl-group sound were Detroit's Motown Records and New York City's Brill Building, in which songwriting teams such as Carole King and Gerry Goffin and Jeff Barry and Ellie Greenwich churned out songs for these teenage girls to sing. Some were sunny, fluffy tunes such as "Goin' to the Chapel" (recorded by the Dixie Cups) and "One Fine Day" (by the Chiffons). But they also wrote darker, more conflicted offerings for the groups, often turning their tragic moments into lyrical fodder. (The Crystals' 1962 recording "He Hit Me [And It Felt Like a Kiss]," for one, was based on the abusive relationship of Little Eva, who was Carole King's baby sitter and who later had a hit with "The Loco-Motion.") The Shirelles' "Will You Love Me Tomorrow?", a number-one hit in 1960, featured a narrator ready to succumb to some backseat ardor but grappling with the imagined consequences. Singer Skeeter Davis's "I Can't Stay Mad at You" painted a frankly masochistic (if musically upbeat) portrait of a girl so in love with her boyfriend that no amount of bad-boy shenanigans can turn her away. And teenage vocalist Lesley Gore offered

The Ronettes (consisting of Veronica Bennett, her sister Estelle Bennett, and their cousin Nedra Talley) were one of the most popular girl groups of the early 1960s.

a protest against an overbearing beau with "You Don't Own Me." Though her voice was soft and sweet, she wasn't fooling around when she demanded that her guy not boss her around and treat her like just another of his belongings.

Would these girl groups have written different songs for themselves had they been given the chance? It's worth wondering. Because as iconic as these groups' sounds and looks became—the Ronettes with their ratted-up, gravity-defying beehives, the Shangri-Las with their leather jackets and heavy eyeliner, the Supremes and their Vegas sequins— they were still the creation (and the music the literal property) of men. Still, in these images and songs, many women found their own voices. As Susan J. Douglas writes of these groups: "The main purpose of pop music is to make us feel a kind of euphoria that convinces us that we can transcend the shackles of conventional life and rise above the hordes of others who do get trapped. It is the euphoria of commercialism, designed to get us to buy. But this music did more than that; it generated another kind of euphoria as well. For when tens of millions of young girls starting feeling, at the same time, that they, as a generation, would not be trapped, there was planted the tiniest seed of a social movement."

As the target audience for pop music—as opposed to more "serious" forms such as jazz and folk—girls were both desired (for the money they spent on records) and derided (for their putatively unsophisticated, faddish tastes). The phrase "teenybopper," though originally coined to describe slavish young followers of any cultural fad, became specific to girl fans of pop music in the mid-'60s. But though teen girls had long swooned over Hollywood pinups and TV actors, their access to live music gave a more urgent, more sexual flavor to their fandom, one that clearly frightened cultural onlookers. On the Beatles' first American tour, the story of four young men in a new band from London who had crossed the pond to play their instruments became secondary to the story of the teen and preteen girls who greeted them—girls who were screaming and weeping and scaling police barriers in their addled lust.

In their essay from the 1992 anthology *The Adoring Audience: Fan Culture and Popular Media* titled "Beatlemania: Girls Just Want to Have Fun," Barbara Ehrenreich, Elizabeth Hess, and Gloria Jacobs posit that Beatlemania was a landmark moment of collective consciousness for teen girls—a movement in which their screams were heard not just aurally but politically as the drumbeat of sexual revolution. It sounds like a stretch, but the writers make a convincing argument:

> *The screaming ten- to fourteen-year-old fans of 1964 did not riot for anything. . . . But they did have plenty to riot against. . . . [T]een and preteen girls were expected to be not only 'good' and 'pure' but to be the enforcers of purity within their teen society—drawing the line for overeager boys and ostracizing girls who failed in this responsibility. To abandon control—*

to scream, faint, dash about in mobs—was in form if not in consious intent, to protest the sexual repressiveness, the rigid double standard of female teen culture. It was the first and most dramatic uprising of women's sexual revolution.

The singers Frank Sinatra, Elvis, and Fabian, among others, had incited manic girl fandom as well, but Beatlemania was somehow different. Remember that male gaze? Well, the hysteria of Beatlemania was perhaps the first instance of a mass *female* gaze—women looking for their own pleasure, men only too conscious of being looked at. It's worth arguing that Beatlemaniacs desperately wanted to be seen by their individual Beatle crush—most girls identified as a "Paul girl," a "John girl," and so on—but even if that's true, it doesn't minimize the force with which their collective gaze sought to devour the band. Who knows what made the Beatles different from Frank or Elvis or Fabian? Maybe it was their foreign-yet-still-accessible Britishness, or the unaffected joy of their bobble-headed, mop-topped stage presence, or the fact that the Beatles in their early incarnation still offered a sweet, lovesick androgyny for girls who weren't yet ready to cross the bridge between cosseted girlhood and sexual womanhood.

In her memoir *I'm with the Band: Confessions of a Groupie*, Pamela Des Barres recalls the Beatlemania that seized her as a teen and the moment when her female gaze was returned by one of the Beatles themselves. After camping out at the band's Bel Air hotel, she writes, "On the way down the hill, a limousine passed by, and I saw John Lennon for an instant. He was wearing his John Lennon cap and he looked right at me. If I close my eyes for an instant, I can still see the look he had on his face; it was full of sorrow and contempt. The other girls were pooling tears in their eyes and didn't notice, but that look on John Lennon's face stopped my heart and I never said a word."

That look of sorrow and contempt says so much about how female music fandom was—and in many ways, still is—marginalized. Music such as the Beatles'—and later, that of equally squeal-inducing outfits such as the Bay City Rollers, Menudo, and *NSYNC—was marketed almost exclusively to teen girls, and though those girls went reliably crazy for it, they were still derided for doing so by bands and critics and promoters. The subtext—filled in by music critics through the years—was that making music for girls was a profitable, but not artistic, pursuit. Even today, you'd be hard-pressed to find a male music fan to give more than a perfunctory nod to *Meet the Beatles*. He would surely protest that the band's really valuable, artistic work came later, with *The White Album*, perhaps, after the girls had moved on and the band members were no longer mop-topped sweethearts playing to a crowd.

It's this enduring characterization in music—men make the records, girls swoon for the bands—that led new generations of female fans to become musicians themselves. Many female musicians of the 1970s, '80s, and '90s would describe their preteen and teen music fandom as a revelation, the moment they realized they wanted to *be* the star on stage, not just look at or be loved by the star on stage. The experience of music fandom changed their perspective, and the female gaze changed their lives. Though Beatlemania and its legacy is rarely linked with the birth of second wave feminism, it told of a restlessness and a stirring in women across America, one that would soon have a formal airing in the culture at large.

Naming the Problem with No Name: Feminism and Pop Culture

Betty Friedan's landmark work *The Feminine Mystique* began its life as a questionnaire sent by Friedan to her fellow alumna of Smith College's class of 1942 fifteen years after they graduated. Their responses to her open-ended questions about how well their educations had prepared them for careers both in and outside the home so surprised her that she worked up an article that she pitched to, in turn, *Ladies' Home Journal*, *McCall's*, and *Redbook*. All of them refused to publish what Friedan wrote. But the more she researched and talked to women who found themselves unfulfilled by life—and certain that their own individual failings and neuroses were to blame—the more she realized that there was a profound need to make women's private fears into a public dialogue.

The feminine mystique, as Friedan coined it, was a definition of womanhood that had little to do with the woman herself. She was defined by her husband as "wife," by her children as "mother," and by commercial forces as a consumer of various personal and household goods that supposedly gave her a sense of self and purpose. And the "problem with no name" identified by the book was a paradox: that a woman who had gotten everything she was supposed to want—the husband, the kids, the split-level ranch house with its two-car garage and gleaming kitchen fixtures—felt a persistent sense of letdown, a resounding inner echo of the question "Is that it?"

In a new introduction to the 2001 edition of *The Feminine Mystique*, Friedan elaborated: "I called it 'the problem that had no name' because women were blamed then for a lot of problems—not getting the kitchen sink white enough, not pressing the husband's shirt smooth enough, the children's bedwetting, the husband's ulcers, their own lack of orgasm. But there was no name for a problem that had nothing to do with husband, children, home, sex."

In not merely identifying the results of women's oppression but naming the root causes of it, *The Feminine Mystique* hit the consciousness of white, middle-class women like a sonic boom, perching on bestseller lists for most of the spring and summer of 1963. Women whose reading material tended toward romance novels and recipe books were suddenly running out to buy this radical text. Its reception among those women—confused, relieved, and furious women—is credited with kicking off the women's movement that coalesced several years after the book's publication.

But like those women's-magazine editors who refused to publish Friedan's original article, the culture at large was wary of giving her theories too much credence. This isn't to say that the media hadn't noticed the growing epidemic of dissatisfaction among middle-class women. Journalist May Craig startled the nation at a 1960 press conference by asking President Kennedy what he was doing for women. (Kennedy wasn't quite sure—and, to his credit, established a Presidential Commission on the Status of Women the next year, with Eleanor Roosevelt at the helm;

the Equal Pay Act was passed two years later.) Friedan herself noted in *The Feminine Mystique* that such publications as *Newsweek*, the *New York Times*, and *Good Housekeeping* were running pieces on housewifely woes in 1960. But none of these outlets were digging deep enough, preferring instead to chalk up the problem to an excess of education ("The road from Freud to Frigidaire, from Sophocles to Spock, has turned out to be a bumpy one," wrote the *New York Times*) or too much freedom of mind (a male *Harper's Bazaar* writer in 1960, in an attempt at levity, suggested that women's right to vote should be revoked, as "Today a woman has to make both the family and the political decisions, and it's too much for her"). Elsewhere, articles with manifesto-like titles such as "Our Greatest Waste of Talent is Women" hinted that a whiff of change was in the air.

Still, to focus, as Friedan did, not on symptoms of the problem but on the entire system that created that problem—well, no media outlet wanted to rock *that* boat. And so, as the women's movement got under way in the latter years of the 1960s, popular culture was both the key to spreading its message and the force that did its damnedest to undermine it.

Through advertising, advice columns, television, and music, pop culture had for decades played a crucial role in dictating to women who they were, who they should aspire to be, what they wanted, who they wanted, what was good, and what was bad. So it makes sense that pop culture was the site of the first large-scale feminist actions, actions in which the lies and machinations of the media and of pop products were deconstructed and laid bare for everyone to see—everyone, that is, who wanted to see.

The first of these actions was the No More Miss America protest, the brainchild of a loose assemblage of writers, activists, and artists who called themselves New York Radical Women. Many of these women had come out of the civil rights movement, the movement opposing the war in Vietnam, and organizations such as Students for a Democratic Society. Disenchanted with the sexism they found there, they sought to address women's oppression as a systemic problem that affected every aspect of public and private life. Whereas organizations such as the

National Organization for Women (NOW) and the National Women's Political Caucus (NWPC)—which would come to be known as part of "liberal feminism"—lobbied to change a patriarchal system by way of antidiscrimination laws, pay equity, and the election of women to public office, self-described "radical feminists" saw the system itself as the problem. Radical-feminist groups (among them the Redstockings, the Feminists, WITCH, Cell 16, and the Furies) didn't want to share power with men—they wanted to create a new system that wasn't about power at all. In their consciousness-raising groups, speakouts, and broadsides (published essays and calls to action), radical feminists aimed to articulate that women's equality would come about only through direct and confrontational action. Simply put, the goal of liberal feminism was to get women a place at the male, capitalist, meritocratic table; the goal of radical feminism was to demolish the table itself. As a result, there was a distinct uneasiness between these two threads of the feminist movement, which was made more pronounced by NOW's fear that lesbians in the group's midst—the so-called "lavender menace"—would compromise the organization's message.

The Miss America protest typified radical feminism. Held in 1968 on the boardwalks of Atlantic City, the action was a mixture of outrage, education, and biting humor. The idea was simple: As the group's No More Miss America! manifesto put it, the women were gathering to protest not that specific pageant but rather "the image of Miss America, an image that oppresses women in every area it purports to represent us." (Given that Miss America and beauty queens in general have become something of a cultural punch line these days, it seems important to point out here that a Miss America crown was for many years considered the most prestigious title any woman could hold; in the early 1960s, the pageant telecast was among the highest-rated shows on TV.) Their ten-point protest included statements about the racist, sexist, and commercial nature of the pageant and the title, as well as about the use of Miss America by the United States as a "military death mascot" whose promotional appearances invariably included trips abroad to raise the spirits of soldiers.

Protesters at the 1968 Miss America pageant used humor and art to express their out-rage at the contest's racism, sexism, commercialism, and oppression of women.

The plan for the day was simple, freewheeling, and even kind of joyous: New York Radical Women envisioned a protest that would culminate in a women's liberation rally to coincide with the crowning of the new Miss America, but that would also be, as NYRW put it, "a groovy day on the boardwalk." More than one hundred protesters showed up, with handmade signs bearing slogans such as "Miss America is a big falsie," and "I am not somebody's pet, toy, or mascot." One demonstrator had rented a live sheep, which protesters decorated with a blue rosette and crowned Miss America. And there was the now-famous Freedom Trash Can, into which the women tossed their girdles, false eyelashes, stiletto heels ("high heels mean low status!"), and, of course, their bras.

The event drew lots of attention from boardwalk bystanders, and their reactions offered plenty of evidence of why the protest was needed in the first place. In Susan Brownmiller's *In Our Time: Memoir of a Revolution*, New York Radical Woman Leah Fritz recalls how onlookers catcalled the women: "They were alternating, 'Hey, good-lookin'—watcha doing tonight?' with 'Boy, get a load of that one—what a dog!' . . . The men acted as if we were conducting a beauty contest. I'd never felt such humiliation."

Indeed, passing judgment on the demonstrators themselves, rather than on the demonstrations, would quickly become a motif of the media's coverage of women's liberation. And though the Miss America pageant was greeted with some positive and sympathetic coverage in places such as *Life* magazine and the *New York Times*, more coverage focused on the loud, unladylike women who had dared to speak up.

The second pop culture–centered action of women's liberation was conceived by an activist group called Media Women, peopled by journalists, filmmakers, and screenwriters. These women and others were gratified to see a surge in homemade, underground media made by women's liberation crusaders, including the publications *No More Fun and Games*, *Everywoman*, and *off our backs*. But they were also frustrated that mainstream women's magazines seemed to have no idea that women's roles were changing. Run by men and bursting with perky tips and male-issued directives on how to keep the cleanest house and have the happiest marriage, magazines such as *Good Housekeeping*, *McCall's*, and *Ladies' Home Journal* were stuck in a 1950s ideal and intent on keeping women there with them. In *In Our Time*, Media Women member Brownmiller describes the "deceitful ideology" presented in women's magazines: "In a make-believe world of perfect casseroles and Jell-O delights, marriages failed because women didn't try hard enough, single-parent households did not exist, and women worked outside the home not because they wanted to, or to make ends meet, but to 'earn extra income in your spare time.'"

Media Women decided that a sit-in—in which the members would literally occupy the offices of a magazine and demand an audience with its top brass—was their best bet both for press coverage (reporters and photographers would be invited in advance to the action) and for getting their voices heard. So in March 1970, the women infiltrated *Ladies' Home Journal* in professional dress, blending in with the writers

A Burning Question, Answered

BRA BURNER.

It's been a shorthand description of modern feminism for countless years. If you were to check the *New York Times* archives and search for the term "bra burning" in all articles published since 1981, you'd turn up handfuls of articles, all using the phrase either as an adjective to describe feminism and feminist-type activities or as a direct synonym for feminism. On LexisNexis, a search for "bra burning" and "feminism" in articles from 2006 and 2007 turns up fifty side-by-side mentions of the two.

The only problem? Only three of the articles found on LexisNexis—and none of those from the *New York Times*—mention that bra burning is perhaps the biggest myth of modern feminism. In all the rest, the myth is simply furthered through rote repetition. It's been repeated as fact in nearly every mainstream forum in which feminism is debated, debunked, and demeaned. But where did the equation between women's lib and flaming undergarments begin? And more important, why has it persisted for such a long, annoying time? Let's parse one before we get to the other.

The 1968 Miss America protest on the boardwalks of Atlantic City was a milestone of women's liberation activism, but perhaps its greater legacy is that it was ground zero for the feminists-as-bra-burners legend. In the official manifesto for the event, the organizers boasted that amid picket lines, guerrilla theater, and leafleting, the protest would also feature "a huge Freedom Trash Can (into which we will throw bras, girdles, curlers, false eyelashes, wigs, and representative issues of *Cosmopolitan*, *Ladies' Home Journal*, *Family Circle*, etc.—bring any such woman-garbage you have around the house). . . ." The Freedom Trash Can was, in the original plan, supposed to be set ablaze, but as the protesters were unable to secure a fire permit for the event—and presumably felt that protesting Miss America was plenty of civil disobedience for one day—they simply invited their cohorts to dump, rather than burn, their feminine trappings.

A little perspective here seems important: Undergarments these days are mass fashion—in many places high fashion—and plenty of women treat their underthings not as boring-yet-necessary staples but as an extension of the rest of their wardrobes. But in the 1960s there was no Victoria's Secret, Agent Provocateur, or American Apparel making undies seem like sexy, fun, optional, and comfortable fripperies. Bras, girdles, and—*oof*—nylon hose were both restrictive and compulsory for women in professional settings, and dumping these underpinnings really was a tangible act of defiance. (The 1950s- and '60s-era bras in particular appear to be alien cousins of today's designed-to-look-natural styles; elaborately cantilevered, their cups ringed with rigid stitching, they imprisoned their wearer's breasts into gravity-defying cones.) Throwing away what author Germaine Greer famously called "a ludicrous invention" was just one piece of a larger rejection of the expectations placed on women.

But back to the birth of that nutty myth. For many years, it was assumed that the titillating image of incinerated unmentionables—and the scandal of free-boobing gals running wild in the streets—was invented by a scornful male reporter covering the Miss America protest from afar. But in a 1992 issue of *Ms.*, contributing editor Lindsy Van Gelder fessed up: As a young reporter covering the protest for the *New York Post*, Van Gelder was the unwitting author of the myth. Her article "Bra Burners and Miss America" was an attempt to draw parallels between women's actions at the No More Miss America! protest and another form of resistance at the time—young men's burning their draft cards to protest the Vietnam War. But sadly, that nuance was lost as other outlets picked up on the racy imagery.

Van Gelder's piece ran in the *Post* a few days before the protest; picking up on the headline, her colleague Harriet Van Horne let loose two days after it with a furious piece headlined "Female Firebrands." Though Van Horne didn't attend the event or speak with any of the women involved, she nevertheless painted a fearsome picture: "With screams of delight, [protesters] consigned to the flames such shackling, demeaning items as girdles, bras, high-heeled slippers, hair curlers, and false eyelashes," she wrote, before going on to label the protesters "unstroked, uncaressed, and emotionally undernourished." Syndicated columnist Art Buchwald piled on a few days later with a column titled "Uptight Dissenters Go Too Far in Burning Their Brassieres," and the myth was quickly cemented.

and secretaries in the magazine's New York offices. They had come prepared with a list of demands: a female editor-in-chief "who is in touch with women's real problems and needs," the hiring of nonwhite women at all levels in the magazine's operations, a raise in salary, free daycare facilities, no more articles directly tied to advertising, and no more advertising that degraded women. In addition, they demanded that the magazine "use women writers for all columns and freelance assignments because men speak to women through the bias of their male supremacist concepts," and that the *Journal* dispose of its long-running column "Can This Marriage Be Saved?", which put the burden of marriage saving directly on women. (Susan J. Douglas and Meredith W. Michaels, in their 1994 book *The Mommy Myth: The Idealization of Motherhood and How It Has Undermined Women*, suggested this column would be better titled "Will This Wife Eat Shit?") The final item on the list of demands was that the women's liberation movement be allowed to produce all the editorial content of one issue of the *Journal*, with a monthly column to follow thereafter. They had come prepared with lists of ideas for magazine features that would both modernize the editorial coverage and give a nod to the growing women's movement: articles on abortion, divorce, environmental pollution caused by household products, and more.

After an eleven-hour occupation, Media Women and *Ladies' Home Journal* editor and publisher John Mack Carter came to an agreement. It was nowhere as far-reaching as the women had hoped for, but the *Journal* agreed to give Media Women eight editorial pages and ten thousand dollars. Several years later, senior editor Lenore Hershey was appointed editor-in-chief. (As Brownmiller notes, however, at the demonstration Hershey was "a magpie passing judgment on our clothes, our hair, our extremely rude manners," and her appointment as editor didn't necessarily ensure a feminist point of view.)

Still, the demonstration was successful enough that many of the women duplicated it a month later, occupying the office of Grove Press, whose publication of erotica was considered degrading. The women wanted to see profits from the "pornography" published by

Grove used to establish a bail fund for prostitutes, among other things, but this action ended less auspiciously, with nine women arrested and hauled off to jail for the night. Grove Press continued publishing its erotica unimpeded.

By the early 1970s, popular culture was quickly becoming both a locus for feminist organizing and a source of simmering empowerment. Women affixed stickers reading THIS AD INSULTS WOMEN to offending billboards in the subways. Aretha Franklin's "Respect" took Otis Redding's 1950s hit and gave it a righteous gender flip. The so-called sexual revolution encouraged women to cast off their hang-ups, and a growing number of female writers, artists, musicians, and reporters instructed them in how to do so. In the decades to come, popular culture would be cemented as America's common language—and both women's and feminism's place within it got increasingly complicated.

CHAPTER 3

WE HAVEN'T COME A LONG WAY, AND DON'T CALL ME BABY: THE 1970S AND '80S

IN 1968, *ADVERTISING AGE* MAGAZINE reported on the success of two campaigns aimed at getting American women to smoke more cigarettes. One was for Silva Thin, whose campaign employed a kind of psychological come-on in pitching the "impossible cigaret." In TV ads for Silva Thins, the cigarette was smoked not by a woman but by a dashing, mysterious man, who was pictured abandoning women for his tobacco-filled love in various scenic locales. But in positioning the man as unattainable, the ad sought to make women want him—and thus the cigarette—even more.

The other ad campaign praised by the magazine was for Virginia Slims, the first cigarettes made expressly for women. The campaign's pitch was "You've Come a Long Way, Baby," and in print ads for the brand—which ran in nearly every women's magazine on the market— modern gals were pictured kicking up their high heels, looking sassy, and reveling in their good fortune. To illustrate just how far these liberated smokers had come, the ads featured sepia-toned photographs of women in corsets and Gibson-girl hairdos, pictured trying to filch their husbands' cigarettes or steal away for a quick smoke in private.

Was having our own potentially deadly tobacco product really progress? Plenty of women seemed to think so: Parent company Phillip Morris reported moving 1.3 billion cigarettes in Virginia Slims' first three months of national distribution, according to Alice Embree's essay "Media Images I: Madison Avenue Brainwashing—The Facts" in the anthology *Sisterhood Is Powerful: An Anthology of Writings from the Women's Liberation Movement.* And though *Advertising Age* predicted that the Silva Thins campaign would be far more successful than the one for Virginia Slims, it was wrong—it was the latter campaign that won a Clio (the Oscar of the ad industry), and whose tagline has gone on to be a signifier of the commercial appeal of women's liberation.

By the end of the 1960s, the second wave of feminism was crashing onto the shores of Hollywood, Madison Avenue, and pop culture at large, and the result was a cycle of co-optation and backlash that continues to this day. Virginia Slims wasn't the first product whose advertising tried to speak to women in the language of liberation: Maidenform's "Dream" campaign, in which women, naked from the waist up save for their bras, were photographed in public spaces enacting some fantasy activity ("I dreamed I played Cleopatra/went on a tiger hunt/was a knockout in my Maidenform bra"), started its wish-fulfilling life in 1949. But Virginia Slims was the first product that interpreted feminism as a battle of the sexes that could sell. Those sepia insets of old-timey women trying to outsmart their husbands in pursuit of a smoke, juxtaposed with smiling modern ones holding their Slims just so, suggested that women had won. Never mind sexism and the unratified Equal Rights Amendment—we've got cigarettes!

By the early 1970s, feminist critiques of advertising were an indelible part of the movement. On the mainstream, liberal-feminist front, NOW founder Betty Friedan had pilloried the industry in *The Feminine Mystique* for its manipulation of women's desires and its casting of their oppressions—housework, cooking, beauty ideals—as exciting consumer choices. Meanwhile, radical feminists stated that the evil of advertising lay in its desire to make all women into sex objects. In her 1969 article "Women and the Myth of Consumerism," Ellen Willis, former member of New York Radical Women and cofounder, with Shulamith Firestone, of Redstockings, wrote: "In a sense, fashion, cosmetics, and 'feminine hygiene' ads are aimed more at men than at women. They encourage men to expect women to sport all the latest trappings of sexual slavery—

In 1915, Mrs. Cynthia Robinson was caught smoking in the cellar behind the preserves. Although she was 34, her husband sent her straight to her room.

It's different now. Now there's a slim cigarette for women only. New Virginia Slims.

Virginia Slims are slimmer than the fat cigarettes men smoke. They're tailored slim to fit your hands, your lips, and your purse. And blended with the kind of flavor women like. Rich, mild Virginia flavor. Extra long. Light one up.

You've come a long way.

To market its new Virginia Slims brand of cigarettes, Phillip Morris used the language of feminism to appeal to women's sense of progress. The text in the upper right-hand corner of this magazine ad reads: "In 1915, Mrs. Cynthia Robinson was caught smoking in the cellar behind the preserves. Although she was 34, her husband sent her straight to her room."

expectations women must fulfill if they are to survive. . . . One of a woman's jobs in this society is to be an attractive sexual object, and clothes and make-up are tools of the trade."

Citing advertising that was demeaning, infantilizing, and just plain insulting (including ads for Silva Thins), women's groups such as NOW enacted boycotts against the offending products and in so doing made sure a feminist critique of the industry echoed beyond their own circles. By the mid-1970s, the National Advertising Review Board had responded, appointing a panel to assess ads either directed to or portraying women and drawing up a list of questions for advertisers to consult when creating campaigns, including ones such as "Do my ads portray women as more neurotic than men?" and "Do my ads portray women actually driving cars?"

That said, cosmetics and fragrance companies wrung their hands at the thought that women and girls, fired up by the rhetoric of women's lib, would simply stop consuming the products they'd been told for years were indispensable—the powder, the lipstick, the hairspray, and the feminine hygiene products. (This fear, in fact, proved to be justified by the end of the decade, with sales of cosmetics and attendance at high-priced salons in a slump.) Their solution was to follow Virginia Slims' lead and use feminism itself as the sales pitch. Thus women got the Liberated Wool Sweater, advertised by the American Wool Council as "the embodiment of the new freedom." They got Revlon's Charlie, a fragrance for "the new woman" launched in 1973; it wasn't clear what was so new about Charlie's woman, other than maybe the fact that she sported pants, but the fragrance quickly became a national bestseller. And they got a whole new range of "natural look" cosmetics designed to make them appear bare faced and beautiful. Women could now look makeup-free without having to actually give up makeup— emancipation, cosmetics industry–style.

Striking Down the Strikers: Feminism in the Media Spotlight

The hurry to add a dash of feminist flavor to existing consumer products was out of step with the way actual feminists were received in the mainstream media during the 1970s. News organizations reporting on the phenomenon of women's liberation described feminists with terminology that alternated between condescending ("libbers") and fearmongering (women described as "militants," the movement itself called "a contagion"), and they spent at least as much time reporting on the dress and hairstyles of feminist women as they did on actual feminist actions and concerns.

Even when trivializing it, the news media made women's liberation one of the biggest stories of the decade. An instructive example is the Women's Strike for Equality, held on August 26, 1970, to celebrate the fiftieth anniversary of women's suffrage. With organized actions and rallies in more than forty states, the strike was conceived as a way to highlight the fact that despite the right to vote, women still had yet to reach equality in work, at home, and in social life. The strike was spearheaded by NOW founder Betty Friedan, who saw the event as the movement's overture to all women, describing it as a "resistance, both passive and active, of all women in America against the concrete conditions of their oppression. . . . In every office, every laboratory, every school, all the women to whom we get word will spend the day discussing and analyzing the conditions which keep us from being all we can be."

The strike was an undeniable success, with more than fifty thousand attendees at the New York event alone, waving placards that read DON'T IRON WHILE THE STRIKE IS HOT, and even draping the Statue of Liberty with a sign reading WOMEN OF THE WORLD UNITE! It was also, simply put, Big News—the first major media event of second wave feminism. The three major broadcast networks provided on-site, live reportage, and the *New York Times*, the *Washington Post*, the *Chicago Tribune*, and other newspapers ran advance front-page coverage.

And yet, plenty of the poststrike coverage aimed to undermine the spirit of the event. The fact that Friedan was late to the rally because of a holdup at the hair salon, for instance, was magnified in a *New York Times* piece titled "Leading Feminist Puts Hairdo Before Strike." ABC's report on the event was condescending from the jump, opening with an amused quote from then-Vice President Spiro Agnew ("Three things have been difficult to tame: the oceans, fools, and women. We may soon be able to tame the oceans, but fools and women will take a little longer.") and closing with an even more dismissive one from a West Virginia senator calling the women's movement a "small band of braless bubbleheads." (The quote ran on the other two networks as well, making it the sound bite of the day.)

Unsurprisingly, almost none of the news organizations that covered the Women's Strike for Equality asked for quotes from women actually involved in the event, preferring to seek out women who asserted that they themselves didn't feel the least bit oppressed. Yet another *New York Times* piece, headlined "Traditional Groups Prefer to Ignore Women's Lib," interviewed members of traditional women's organizations such as the Daughters of the American Revolution and the Junior League and found that these genteel ladies considered those wacky women's libbers to be "unattractive," "communists," and "a band of wild lesbians." It's true that many radical feminist groups were hostile to the media, preferring not to seek coverage that would invariably be negative. But liberal feminist groups, especially NOW, saw the media as a necessary tool with which to spread the word of the women's movement, and they made themselves readily available for quotes and interviews via newsletters and press releases. But as with coverage of such movements as the student antiwar effort and the black power movement, the press reaction seemed to be one of primarily "writing around" the issues rather than going directly to the people most closely involved for quotes.

Why were so many people intent on discrediting the idea that women should have the same social standing and opportunities as men? In a country that had literally been founded on the revolt of one group against its rulers, why was the reality of women fighting for those opportunities so frightening not only to men but to other women? Part of the answer was simply that political and social-justice movements in America were invariably viewed as zero-sum propositions. You oppose the war in Vietnam? Well, then you're anti-American. You're all for black power? Gee, I guess you hate white people. You support women's equality? That must mean you want to bring men down. This simplistic public gloss on these movements and their adherents simply didn't allow for a full understanding of why such movements resonated with a cross-section of people; all they did was whip folks into a frenzy by conjuring the specter of lost power for the dominant group.

But specific to spectators of the women's liberation movement was skepticism of its very premise. Plenty of folks were quick to protest that women who agitated for more rights were simply being petty, their demands born of a refusal to just settle down and enjoy their inherent, biological inferiority to men. In a broadcast the day before the strike, ABC anchor Howard K. Smith stated confidently that women were equal already, given that they made up 50 percent of the population— an assertion that made about as much sense as concluding that a pile of one-dollar bills had the same value as a pile of fifties so long as there were the same number of them. Smith's reasoning was made even more ridiculous when he added that women "get the most money, inherited from worn-out husbands." The kind of fact-based reporting normally demanded by major news networks was, in the run-up to the strike, replaced by pure subjective reaction and speculation. Liberated women, newsmakers worried, would abandon their children and refuse to cook or do laundry for their families, short-circuiting the accepted domestic machinery. They'd make a mockery of the armed forces and of traditionally male workplaces by displacing men who'd "earned" the right to be there. And most horrifying of all, they'd defeminize themselves, refusing to pretty up their surroundings or smile on cue. If the measure of women's oppression was men's resistance to their liberation, as Pat Mainardi wrote in her 1970 essay "The Politics of Housework," the reaction to the Women's Strike for Equality revealed a female populace that, indeed, was mightily oppressed.

In the wake of the Women's Strike for Equality, mainstream media outlets seemed obsessed by feminism and feminist personalities—who were these self-possessed women? Where had they come from? Why did they think they could challenge the status quo? And, most important, were they married and did they shave their legs? This attack-dog approach set the tone for decades of future coverage of feminist issues and actions, in which news outlets reported on feminism without talking to actual feminists, letting a few choice words from self-professed "anti-women's-libbers" define the entire movement. Reporter Marilyn Goldstein of *Newsday* revealed that a male editor assigned her to report on the women's movement with the directive, "Get out there and find an authority who'll say this is all a crock of shit."

And yet plenty of people saw through this hostile agenda to the true aims of the movement and joined up: NOW's membership alone grew from twelve hundred to forty-eight thousand between 1967 and 1974. Perhaps it was even the transparent sexism of the coverage itself that led many people to feminism; if the media frenzy surrounding the women's strike made anything clear, it was that feminism seemed like enough of a threat to justify entire newscasts and newspaper stories insisting that it wasn't.

In part to counteract the media's ignorance and willful misrepresentation of feminism, feminist activists became wildly prolific, conveying the experiences and urgency of women's liberation through writing and publishing. By 1972, there were two categories of women's-movement literature. There was the publishing of feminism— books written and edited by movement participants such as Kate Millett, Shulamith Firestone, and Robin Morgan and published by storied establishment houses. And there was feminist publishing: zines, newsletters, and books written by women, for women, and published on shoestring budgets. By 1972, zines such as *Spare Rib* and *It Ain't Me, Babe*, newsletters such as *Notes from the First Year* and *The Majority Report*, and books such as the Boston Women's Health Book Collective's *Our Bodies, Ourselves* were part of a burgeoning underground. Some of these publications served as documentation of the women's liberation movement, reprinting speeches, manifestos, and transcripts of conversations between women in the movements; others were more like guidebooks introducing outsiders to the concept of women's liberation. *Our Bodies, Ourselves*—which started as a pamphlet titled *Women and Their Bodies*—served both purposes, with its sisterly use of the language of empowerment aimed at combating the deeply paternalistic state of women's healthcare and encouraging women to join with others in framing specifically female-focused healthcare as a feminist issue.

The 1971 preview issue of a new magazine called *Ms.* hoped to be a bridge between the publishing of feminism and feminist publishing. Though ideologically closer to the latter category, as a glossy magazine

Ms. was also in the former, working within existing industry channels to bring feminism to a mass-market audience. The preview issue, which appeared as an insert in *New York* magazine, borrowed the service-oriented tone of women's magazines such as *Redbook* and *Good Housekeeping*, but instead of articles about cheesecake recipes or vacuuming tips, *Ms.* boasted titles such as "How to Write Your Own Marriage Contract" and "Rating the Candidates: Feminists Vote the Rascals In or Out."

Less than a year later, *Ms.* was launched as a stand-alone periodical, complete with a cover featuring feminist superhero Wonder Woman and an article on her legacy by magazine cofounder Gloria Steinem. For women who had been in the movement for years, *Ms.* was, depending on whom you asked, either a much-needed alternative to women's magazines or the emblem of the second wave's capitalist sellout to the Man. But outside it, in cities and suburbs and rural areas where women had never seen a speculum demonstration or a speakout, *Ms.* was a revelation. In her review of the first issue in *off our backs*, Onka Dekkers gleefully imagined what effect the magazine could have on unsuspecting readers: "There is a female mind-set on those glossy pages slipping into American homes concealed in grocery bags like tarantulas on banana boats. Curious girl children will accidentally discover feminism in *Ms.* the way we stumbled onto sex in our mother's *Ladies Home Journal.*"

Ms., like the women's movement itself, was greeted by mainstream media outlets with a mixture of scorn and dismissal: Notoriously chauvinist TV anchor Harry Reasoner boasted that he would "give it six months before they run out of things to say." But women themselves welcomed *Ms.* with overwhelming support: The preview issue sold out within eight days of its publication, and it garnered more than twenty thousand letters to the editor and as many subscriptions. Of course, a bevy of criticism also came *Ms.*'s way: Plenty of women pointed out that there wasn't enough coverage of women of color, lesbians, blue-collar women, disabled women, older women. As the first national, glossy periodical for feminists, *Ms.* couldn't help but be expected to be all things to all women. But as *off our backs* predicted, *Ms.* would

Ms. *magazine featured Wonder Woman on its inaugural cover in 1972.*

quickly start sneaking feminism into the living rooms and doctor's offices of women who never knew they were in need of it.

One of *Ms.*'s first—and, through its lifetime, hardest—hurdles was the question of advertising. The premier issue featured some of the same ads women saw in "regular" women's magazines, for suntan lotion and cigarettes and assorted other girl stuff. As Steinem wrote in her 1990 essay "Sex, Lies, and Advertising," she and her cofounders saw ads as a tactical move. First, they wanted to keep the magazine affordable. But as important was their desire to "provid[e] a forum where women and advertisers could talk to each other and improve advertising itself. After all, it was (and still is) as potent a source of information in this country as news or TV and movie dramas."

Somewhat trickier was the fact that the *Ms.* collective also wanted to break with the long (if not exactly noble) tradition of "complementary copy" in women's magazines. Complementary copy went something like this: If Nabisco wanted to advertise its piecrust, the editors had to find a way to supplement the ad with some helpful content about that piecrust. Voilà: a two-page spread on all the delicious dinners that could be made with Nabisco's fabulous piecrust. The flip side of this was that if that same magazine ran a piece on how piecrust was unhealthy, the sponsor was pretty much guaranteed to pull out of the next issue.

So for *Ms.*, a magazine whose very point was to critique a system that encouraged women to consume first and think second, this was trouble. The magazine tangled with its sponsor Clairol after printing a short report on the possible carcinogens in hair dyes; Revlon refused to advertise after *Ms.* ran a cover image of women who, horror of horrors, weren't wearing makeup. And in an industry in which faces of color were almost nonexistent as both editorial and advertising models—no women's magazine featured a black cover model until a 1968 issue of *Glamour*, *Vogue* didn't feature a woman of color on its cover until 1974—*Ms.* found companies confused when the magazine's publishers requested advertisements featuring black, Latina, and Asian women. And when *Ms.*'s editors and publishers solicited ads from companies that produced goods traditionally aimed at men—for instance, cars and electronics—they were rebuffed because, as Steinem recalled hearing over and over, "women don't understand technology."

Trying to slot feminism into the conventional framework of the magazine industry was itself an act of consciousness-raising, but unfortunately it was one that exhausted *Ms.*; in 1990, it would switch to an ad-free model and then back to ads several years later. *Ms.*'s hope of an ongoing dialogue between women and advertisers is still out there, and thousands of women have attempted to keep that dialogue going in both individual and collective ways, with protests, letter-writing campaigns, and "girlcotts."

Libbers and Killers: Feminism on the Big Screen

The restrictive Hays Code was lifted in 1968 and was replaced by the Motion Picture Association of America's letter-ratings system. In theory, the letter system implied that films could show almost anything they wanted to (though the dreaded X rating was avoided by most directors and soon became the exclusive province of porn films). Perhaps because of this shift, the 1970s is often considered a kind of golden age of Hollywood filmmaking, in which directors tackled gritty, edgy, real-life subject matter in inventive ways. And that's true, but inevitably, those directors were male, and the gritty, edgy, real-life subjects they tackled were almost always about men. Men on motorcycles (*Easy Rider*), men in gangs (*The Godfather, Mean Streets*), men at war (*Apocalypse Now, The Deer Hunter*), men as vigilantes (*Dirty Harry, Straw Dogs, Shaft*), men battling nature (*Jaws*), and men in dysfunctional buddy relationships (*Midnight Cowboy, Butch Cassidy and the Sundance Kid*). In the pantheon of 1970s classics, women held supporting roles as wives, girlfriends, and prostitutes, if they appeared at all.

Yet the second wave of feminism did inspire a clutch of films during the 1970s that sought to illustrate both cultural fears of women's liberation and women's own ambivalence about seeking domestic emancipation. *Up the Sandbox,* released in 1972, is one such film. Based on the novel by feminist author Anne Roiphe, it starred Barbra Streisand as Margaret, a New York housewife who seems perfectly happy with her life as a wife and mother. And yet, when she finds that she's pregnant with her third child, she suddenly starts slipping into fantasies in which she's an incendiary spokeswoman for feminism, a Black Panther-esque radical planting bombs in the Statue of Liberty, and an anthropologist studying the fertility rites of an African matriarchy. Little context was given for these fantasies, but each scenario seemed as glamorous, dangerous, and radical as Margaret herself was not.

Up the Sandbox was a film that gave voice to Betty Friedan's "problem with no name," both directly and indirectly—in one fantasy sequence, a Fidel Castro manqué delivers a speech denouncing the fact that "middle-class women are treated like slaves. . . . How can children have dignity if their mothers are stripped of it?"; in another scene, Margaret walks in on her husband lunching with a glamorous female colleague and is entranced, as though seeing a vision of what she herself might have been. The end of the film isn't exactly a blow for women's liberation—we can assume that Margaret stays with her husband, has that third baby, and maybe continues to fantasize a more exciting life. But the fact that the film even bothered to critique the limitations of women's roles was both novel and crucial. The same could be said of 1970's *Diary of a Mad Housewife* and, in a decidedly more bizarre take, 1975's *The Stepford Wives,* both of which centered on the lives of female protagonists chafing at the patriarchy embodied by their husbands and communities. Meanwhile, 1974's *Alice Doesn't Live Here Anymore* and 1978's *An Unmarried Woman* offered heroines made stronger and more self-sufficient through divorce but also paired them up with new male partners by movie's end—a Hollywood resolution whose suggestion was that women became liberated not through their own self-actualization but by trading in bad men for better ones.

Movies such as these were the 1970s answer to the women's pictures of the '30s and '40s. Although they swapped melodrama for outrage, they presented stories—about women seeking independence, triumphing over insensitive husbands, and valuing sexual satisfaction over wifely duty—that, it was assumed, would not interest men. On the other end of the spectrum was the cinemachismo of *Taxi Driver*, *Easy Rider*, and others. Somewhere in the middle, there was the female-vengeance film, which plugged a hint of feminism into action and horror genres in ways meant to be entertaining for men and resonant to women.

Vengeance films offered a central character who has either been wronged herself or has seen someone close to her wronged; in response, she takes revenge on the bad guys (who are, invariably, guys) in inventively gruesome ways. Some of the most memorable starred Pam Grier. Known these days as Kit on *The L Word*, Grier was the first female star of the "blaxploitation" genre, and her signature heroine was blunt, black, and stacked. In 1973's *Coffy*, she played a nurse who moonlights as a one-woman task force on street crime, vowing to bring down the system that got her sister hooked on drugs. Packing razor blades in her hair as she went undercover to seduce and destroy, Coffy was, as the movie's poster bragged, "The baddest One-Chick Hit-Squad that ever hit town!" (Posters also noted that "She'll cream ya!") In 1974, *Foxy Brown* offered a similar character, a woman who turns vigilante after her boyfriend is murdered by a lawless gang. The fact that Foxy infiltrates the gang in the guise of a prostitute made for scenes that were sexy, heavy with dread, and that usually didn't end too well for her male targets.

These films were successful in part because (no disrespect to Grier's acting chops) they swapped a gorgeous woman into what was recognizably a man's role: that of an ultraviolent, no-apologies badass. Blaxploitation films, set primarily in urban ghettos and featuring

Stepford Revisited

As an allegory for a growing fear of feminism, it doesn't get much better than the 1975 film *The Stepford Wives*. The movie, based on Ira Levin's 1972 novel of the same name, tells the story of Joanna Eberhardt, a New York City photographer and mother of two, whose husband persuades her to leave the city for the gentler, greener suburb of Stepford, Connecticut. But something's a little off in this pretty town where the lawns are manicured and the living is easy: Joanna soon starts to notice that its wives are a bit, well, robotic. And after a bit of sleuthing around with her new friend Bobbie, Joanna discovers Stepford's chilling secret—a "Men's Association" that is killing off its members' wives and replacing them with pliant, brain-free, sexually submissive automatons. When her husband joins the association, Joanna quickly becomes its next casualty.

The Stepford Wives neatly distilled the dread that greeted women's liberation into a gripping thriller with shots of pitch-black humor. (In one scene, Bobbie, ruminating on life in Stepford, explains to Joanna, "My problem is that, given complete freedom of choice, I don't *want* to squeeze the goddamn Charmin!") The premise—that men so want to retain their power that they prefer actual robots to flesh-and-blood women—was a heady statement about the perceived reach of women's lib and a ripe target for satire.

But can a satire of a satire work? That was the question posed, indirectly, by the 2004 remake of *The Stepford Wives*, an outing that couldn't decide whether it was a comedy or a thriller, and that ended up being

pimps, drug dealers, and renegade cops as their heroic figures, were controversial because at the same time they gave blacks a significant presence both behind and in front of the camera, their characterizations turned on the most pernicious of stereotypes, with pimp hats, hookers, and inner-city poverty as primary set dressing. It's worth arguing that Grier made such a compelling hero precisely because she fit another of those stereotypes—that of the tough-as-nails black broad who's as violent as her brothers were expected to be but more invitingly sexual to boot.

Flipping the gender of the vigilante hero—and making sure she had neither. In the update, Joanna is a ruthless TV executive who is abruptly downsized and suffers a nervous breakdown. She and her husband retreat to Stepford, where the robot wives were all, like Joanna, once high-powered career women. What ensues is either madcap hilarity (Stepford wives whose mouths act as ATMs) or rank sexism (the Stepford of 2004 has the more effeminate half of a gay couple Stepfordized), depending on your point of view.

Inherent in the very idea of a *Stepford Wives* remake was the suggestion that the sexual politics that was the bedrock of the original had worn away. But it hadn't—the male fear of liberated women that the book and original movie essayed was replaced in 2004 with a fear of successful women who emasculated men with their disinterest in things such as doing dishes and baking brownies. It also reflected some retro wishful thinking: Since the terrorist attacks of 9/11, journalists had crowed triumphantly that women were "opting out" of the workplace for family-oriented lives at home, nesting and shelter magazines were on the rise, and buzz phrases such as "The New Domesticity" heralded casserole baking and scrapbooking as ways to feel safe in a war-plagued world. Meanwhile, cosmetic surgeries were growing both more commonplace and more specific (elbow-plumping, anyone?), pressing the conclusion that any woman could—and, more specifically, should—take advantage of science to be as perfect as she possibly could, even if that meant she ended up looking about as real as the original Stepford automatons. Campy as it tried to be, the 2004 *Wives* ended up skewing far closer to documentary than it did to satire.

no problem using sex as a weapon—ensured that men would show up to watch blaxploitation films; adding a love story for Grier's character and positing her power as feminist drew in the ladies. But non-blaxploitation vengeance flicks made no pretense at balance, instead using graphic scenes of rape and torture to allow male audiences to ogle first, second, and third, and then maybe root for the female lead later. Two of the most brutal were 1972's *Last House on the Left* and 1978's *I Spit on Your Grave*. The latter, often known by the alternate title *Day of the Woman*, told the story of a big-city writer who rents a cabin in a small town and is promptly targeted by the local lowlifes.

The film Coffy, *starring Pam Grier, fit into the "blaxploitation" genre with its sexy, gun-toting, revenge-seeking title character.*

After a brutal gang rape in which she's left for dead, our heroine systematically hunts down and kills each of her tormentors in increasingly gruesome ways. *Last House on the Left* (a loose remake of Ingmar Bergman's 1960 classic *The Virgin Spring*) offered a similar plot, with the difference that it is the parents of the raped and murdered girl who offed the gang of baddies.

It's possible that the male directors of these movies (Wes Craven and Meir Zarchi, respectively) did want to position their female leads as empowered in their vengeance; in the DVD commentary for *I Spit*, Zarchi reveals that he was inspired to make the movie after the disillusioning experience of helping a rape victim report her ordeal to a less-than-helpful police officer. But the sheer amount of sexualized spectacle in both movies' rape scenes—the one in *I Spit* plays out over an agonizing forty-plus minutes—and the fact that those scenes last far longer than the revenge scenes suggests otherwise. (The very idea that the heroine in *I Spit* would have sex with her rapists later in the story, even as a prelude to her revenge, is insultingly far-fetched.) And let's not even get into the fact that *I Spit's* poster featured an image of the shapely rear of its heroine, barely covered by her ripped, dirt-smeared underwear. When *I Spit on Your Grave* was released, *Chicago Sun-Times* film critic Roger Ebert led a campaign against the film, calling it a "vile bag of garbage" and campaigning to get it pulled from

Chicago theaters. (Oddly enough, he loved *Last House on the Left*, giving it four stars.) More recently, critic Luke Y. Thompson pointed out on the review website RottenTomatoes.com, "Defenders of *[I Spit]* have argued that the film is actually pro-woman, due to the fact that the female lead wins in the end, which is sort of like saying that cockfights are pro-rooster because there's always one left standing."

The last woman standing in more conventional horror films was dubbed the Final Girl by film theorist Carol Clover, who in her book *Men, Women, and Chain Saws: Gender in the Modern Horror Film* looked at the genres of slasher films (*Halloween*), female-possession films (*The Exorcist*), and rape-revenge films (hi again, *I Spit on Your Grave*) from a feminist perspective. Refuting the conventional wisdom of critics such as Ebert that such films glorified violence against women, Clover's theory was that they actually demanded that viewers identify with the films' terrorized females (rather than the terrorizing males). And since slasher films in particular were understood to appeal to a male audience, she suggested that this identification could be seen as a form of gender subversion.

Which is all well and good. But another question remains: Why did slasher films and the female victim/avenger character become such a staple of 1970s cinema to begin with? One could certainly argue that the new, almost-anything-goes rating system engendered a new thirst for graphic violence: The more directors were able to show, the more they felt they had to show, pushing the boundaries a little more with each film. But if the genre's popularity in the '70s and '80s indicates anything, it's that the men who made up a large share of its audience got plenty of pleasure out of seeing women terrorized, sexualized, and killed. Was rooting for the final girl simply a device that absolved their prurient kick, a kind of celluloid Hail Mary? Or was the final girl, as Clover theorized, the great equalizer of slasher films, the woman who, in outwitting the killer, forced male viewers to see themselves in her?

The structure of horror films has changed little through time; they still force women, as film theorist Linda Williams writes in her essay "When the Woman Looks," in the 1996 book *The Dread of Difference:*

Gender and the Horror Film, to "bear witness to her own powerlessness in the face of rape, mutilation, and murder." So though the Final Girl character has become a staple of not only horror films, but action and sci-fi as well (Sarah Connor in *The Terminator*, Ellen Ripley of the *Alien* series), the films in which they feature could hardly be said to be pro-woman. Having an adrenaline-pumped female lead overcome her literal demons and save the day—or at least her own life—is simply, to pervert the words of Audre Lorde, trying to dismantle the master's house of horrors with the master's bloody ax. But to this day, Hollywood would prefer to tell us that a woman who escapes death (or, even better, avenges herself by dealing it to others) is a feminist rather than stop making films in which women are terrorized.

Though there were the occasionally juicy individual roles for women in Hollywood film in the 1970s (Jane Fonda as a terrorized call girl in *Klute* and as a veteran's wife in *Coming Home*, Diane Keaton as a gorgeous neurotic in *Annie Hall*, Faye Dunaway's steely, corrupted TV exec in *Network*, Meryl Streep's doomed, working-class whistle-blower in *Silkwood*), very few films mirrored the evolution of women's lib as it developed into the 1980s. So 1980's *9 to 5* filled a definite pop culture void: a movie—a comedy, even—that made the point that sexism was systemic, and that it took women working together to change that system. Made during a time when the phrase "sexual harassment" was newly coined and women everywhere were realizing that a pat on the ass from their employer shouldn't be the norm, the film crammed a whole consciousness-raising group's worth of workplace grievances—discrimination, sexual harassment, male bosses who claimed credit for their female employees' ideas—into its plot. Produced by Jane Fonda's film company, the movie borrowed its title from an existing national network that had been set up to unionize female office workers; naturally, it was careful to address the way that women in the workplace often turned on fellow women in the fear that there was room for only one rather than blaming a system that didn't give priority to their employment to begin with.

The movie's leads (Fonda, Lily Tomlin, and Dolly Parton) were uniformly endearing (and, it has to be said, attractive enough for their feminism to be sympathetic), and its "sexist, egotistical, lying, hypocritical bigot" villain one that many women recognized. The film was a success. Lily Tomlin followed *9 to 5* with a dual role in *The Incredible Shrinking Woman,* which told the story of a housewife exposed to a mix of household chemicals that caused her to shrink to tiny proportions. As a literal illustration of women's still-diminished social status, as well as a critique of an increasingly consumerist American society, the film managed to be, like *9 to 5,* both slapstick and meaningful. And thank goodness for small favors, since a filmic backlash against women's rights began in earnest soon afterward.

Career Girls and Wonder Women: The Televised Feminist

If the raised consciousness of feminism wasn't apparent on the big screen during the 1970s, it was definitely in evidence on the small one. By the early part of the decade, TV critics and academics had pointed out again and again that the supposedly democratic medium wasn't giving women their propers. The not-normally-political *TV Guide* repeatedly wagged its finger at the industry for refusing to rise above characterizations of women as pretty, skinny, dopey, hapless housewives or housewife wannabes, both on network shows and in the commercials that supported them. And women themselves were getting fed up: 75 percent of 120,000 women polled by *Redbook* magazine in 1972 agreed that "the media degrades women by portraying them as mindless dolls."

TV executives, a mostly male bunch, weren't quite sure what to do: They had to acknowledge feminism without alienating advertisers to whom the concept was financial anathema. Thus feminism came to the small screen much like it did to real life—as both a source of strength and a butt of jokes, as caricature and catharsis, striking fear into the hearts (and loins) of male characters and forcing female ones to reconcile their new dreams with their safe, conventional identities. Viewers watched as female characters came slowly to feminism (or at least to their own abilities to enact it in their lives) and learned how to respond to the people around them who preferred that they shut up and look pretty.

The most enduring and endearing of these women was Mary Richards, for seven years the central figure of *The Mary Tyler Moore Show*. *MTM* was a wholly original sitcom, the first in history to introduce a female character whose primary relationship was with neither her family nor her male love interest but with her friends and coworkers. (Not coincidentally, it was also one of the first shows to employ a stable of female writers.) As a thirty-year-old single working woman, Mary acted as a kind of stand-in for the new American female: On one hand, she had left her fiancé, put her job before romance, and made it clear that she would rather spend evenings alone than on a series of bad dates. On the other, she was constantly tasked with office grunt work (typing, getting coffee) and never seemed quite sure of her ability to speak up to her oafish boss and unevolved male coworkers. This combination of girl-next-doorishness and what Mary's boss Lou Grant disgustedly called "spunk" was a palatable way to introduce TV viewers to feminist consciousness, and many viewers were gratified to see Mary embrace her own power more fully as the show aged.

If Mary Richards were the strawberry shortcake of TV feminism—light, delicious, and attractive—Maude Findlay was a big, heaping plate of steak: meaty, tough, and not always appetizing. *Maude* was a spin-off of *All in the Family*, and it shared with that show producer Norman Lear's balance of potent wit and unflinching social realism. Maude herself, played by Bea Arthur, was positioned as the anti-Mary: already successful, financially comfortable, and married four times over. She cared little for social graces; she had no trouble standing up to everyday male chauvinism. Loud, strident, kind of butch, and unconcerned about her hair, she was the embodiment of everything most men (and many women) feared and hated about feminism. But nevertheless, *Maude* was a success, the fourth-highest-rated show of the 1972–73 season. In its six-year run, it hit on a host of controversial issues—racism, classism, birth control, depression, divorce, alcoholism—but its most controversial was a two-part episode titled "Maude's Dilemma," in which the forty-seven-year-old character decides to have an abortion. The plot arc generated a fury of letters from viewers protesting the decision—and indeed, few TV characters since have been allowed to choose abortion in such a straightforward way (see sidebar in Chapter 5).

Yet at the same time that feminism was infiltrating TV programming, so was a backlash against it. In more than a few shows, feminism reared its head as a form of temporary brainwashing that women could be talked out of with the right combination of insult and flattery. In one episode of *All in the Family*, for instance, Archie Bunker's somewhat daft daughter has a moment of raised consciousness that dissipates quickly after she realizes she's not exactly sure what she's talking about. ("We're tired of being exploited by men—tired of you holding us down and keeping us back. And if you continue to exploit us, we're gonna rise up against you someday like our black sisters and our Chicano sisters and I don't even know what I'm saying anymore!") And in the fish-out-of-water sitcoms *Green Acres* and *I Dream of Jeannie*, farmwife Lisa and house genie Jeannie get a load of some women's lib and decide to rebel against their domestic roles. After they fail in a variety of slapstick ways, they realize that—of course!—they're not really oppressed. In fact, they don't have it so bad at all!

And then there was Wonder Woman. The comic book character had been created in 1941 by writer William Marston, who believed that girls needed a positive female role model to counter the comic book status quo of violent masculinity. He wrote of his creation that "Wonder Woman is psychological propaganda for the new type of woman who should, I believe, rule the world. There isn't enough love in the male organism to run this planet peacefully." Wonder Woman's creation myth centered on Paradise Island, a man-free homeland for Amazon women who developed their bodies, minds, and social relationships free from any controlling masculine influence; her magic bracelets were made from feminum, a material found only in the underground mines of the island. Marston deeply believed in women's potential in general—and more specifically, in Wonder Woman's

Getting Our Phil: *Donahue* and the Talk-Show Revolution

As female characters wrestled with feminism on evening sitcoms, a day-time talk show began to bring real women and their issues to the small screen. *The Phil Donahue Show*, which ran from 1967 to 1996, became during the '70s a national forum on which women talked about sex, divorce, loneliness, child rearing, health issues, and reproductive rights. Donahue, a sympathetic former theology student, came to define the decade's unironic "sensitive man." In his very first week of programming, in 1967, Donahue interviewed Madalyn Murray O'Hair, the nation's most controversial atheist, and showed footage of a woman giving birth as part of a show on pregnancy and childbirth. Donahue was genial, almost unassuming, and didn't presume to be an expert; rather, he cruised his studio audience, offering the microphone to his viewers for their own thoughts and opinions. The show was hugely popular with a female audience; by 1974, it was syndicated nationwide and had millions of viewers, an estimated 85 percent of whom were women. In a 1992 interview with the *Los Angeles Times*, Donahue credits this success in part to the fact that *Donahue* took advantage of the shortcomings of other TV shows aimed at women, noting that "we got lucky because we discovered early on that the usual idea of women's programming was a narrow, sexist view."

The beauty of daytime talk shows was that they were cheap and easy to produce; as a result of Donahue's success, the format got ever more

ability to tap it. So it's really tempting to wonder what he thought of his beloved Amazon's move from the comics to the TV.

It started out promisingly. By the time the TV series launched in 1976, Wonder Woman had already been adopted as an emblem of the women's liberation movement, gracing the first cover of *Ms.* and pictured brandishing a speculum for a poster about women and healthcare created by the Feminist Health Centers. Television was just starting to embrace female action stars with *Police Woman*, *Get Christie Love!*, and *Charlie's Angels*, and *Wonder Woman* fit the formula these popular in the 1970s and '80s. Donahue's daily show wasn't all great: He pioneered the cringe-worthy talk-show tradition of freak-scene episodes in which nudists, transvestites, neo-Nazis, and others were trotted out onstage with an eye to boosting ratings. But Donahue was also fearless in hitting on the controversial issues of the day, including abortion, homo- and bisexuality, AIDS, and women's rights. Episodes on various aspects of reproduction were banned by some local affiliates, and according to Donahue's autobiography, the Chicago station WGN refused to air a show on the subject of tubal ligation because it was "too educational for women." When Susan Brownmiller's landmark book on rape, *Against Our Will: Men, Women and Rape*, was published in 1975, she became a recurring guest on the show, bringing to an astounded audience the radical notion that rape was not something that happened to individual women but a systemic, political crime against all women.

As his competitors multiplied—by the late 1980s, hit talk-show hosts included Oprah Winfrey, Sally Jessy Raphael, Jenny Jones, Montel Williams, Morton Downey Jr., and Jerry Springer—*Donahue*'s ratings waned. Most daytime talk shows had become trash-talking spectacles in which guests were crudely heckled by audience members for sleeping with family members, dressing like "hos," wanting to be boys instead of girls, and committing other societal infractions; fistfights and chair throwing became an expected element of broadcasts. The reasoned, if controversial, explorations undertaken by *Donahue* in its earlier years were simply too earnest in this climate. But the show's host is still remembered fondly by feminists—and irately by feminist antagonists—as the man who brought women's issues to daytime.

shows put forth; she was powerful but also beautiful and feminine. And she had a male love interest so no viewers got nervous about the whole Amazon thing.

The first season of the show, set during World War II, was more or less faithful to the comics. Wonder Woman's alter ego, Diana Prince, was an undercover spy working to overthrow the Nazis; though her primary allegiance was to the U.S. war effort, she still stopped in at Paradise Island occasionally to catch up with her sisters. But sadly, ABC dropped the show after its first season, and though CBS was quick to snatch it back up, the resulting version changed everything: It shifted the narrative from the 1940s to the present-day 1970s, never mentioned Paradise Island or Diana's Amazon roots, and perhaps most important, positioned its heroine as a sex symbol above all. As Elana Levine points out in *Wallowing in Sex: The New Sexual Culture of 1970s American Television*, the subtle changes in *Wonder Woman's* theme song said it all:

> In the first version of the series, the jazzy theme song proclaimed, "All the world is waiting for you/ And the power you possess/ In your satin tights/ Fighting for your rights/ And the old red, white, and blue!" In contrast, the second version of the series initially featured these lyrics: "All the world is waiting for you/ And the wonders that you do/ In your satin tights/ Fighting for our rights/ And the old red, white, and blue!" [emphases mine] A third version of the theme song during the CBS years would remove the lyrics altogether, leaving only the catchy "Wonder Woman!" refrain. The shift away from references to Wonder Woman's power or her fight for her own rights demonstrates the decreasing presence of explicitly feminist rhetoric over the series' run.

Though *Wonder Woman* had female writers who themselves were steeped in feminism and consciousness raising, the second version of the show was not unlike its contemporaries in the women-fighting-crime genre; as in *Charlie's Angels* or *The Bionic Woman*, women took their orders from a man, rarely voiced their own goals or desires, and were by design or circumstance costumed in ways that can only be described as male gaze-tastic. That said, even though the series failed to make Wonder Woman live up to Marston's original (and admittedly lofty) hopes, many of the young girls and boys who watched it didn't know that, and to them, Wonder Woman was merely a beautiful superhero who happened to be female. It was a step forward in a decade when every step counted.

From *Free to Be* . . . to MTV

Given music's history as a space of social commentary, it's not surprising that the 1970s kicked off with two movement-defining bits of pop culture. The first was the Australian artist Helen Reddy's 1972 feminist anthem "I Am Woman, Hear Me Roar." It's no wonder that the song, with an opening that referenced the growing women's movement and a dawning feminist consciousness, along with Aretha Franklin's "Respect," quickly became an unofficial anthem of women's lib.

Only months after "I Am Woman" became a *Billboard* number 1, the album and songbook *Free to Be . . . You and Me* was released. The brainchild of *That Girl* actress Marlo Thomas (who would later marry fellow feminist Phil Donahue), the project was an effort to teach children about the limitations of gender roles and encourage them to define "boy" and "girl" for themselves. Thomas teamed up with like-minded entertainers—among them Diana Ross, Alan Alda, Dionne Warwick, and Mel Brooks—for songs such as "Housework," which enlightened its listeners that "The lady who smiles as she scours or scrubs or rubs or washes or wipes or mops or dusts or cleans/ Or whatever she does on our TV screens/ That lady is smiling because she's an actress/ And she's earning money for learning those speeches/ That mention those wonderful soaps and detergents and cleansers and cleaners and powders and pastes and waxes and bleaches." Elsewhere, *Free to Be* offered up antichauvinist ditties such as "William's Doll" and "It's All Right to Cry" (performed by New York Giants defensive tackle Rosey Grier) and enthused that both mommies and daddies "can be anything they want to be." The album was a Grammy-winning hit and went on to be an Emmy-winning TV special; all its proceeds went to the Ms. Foundation.

The rock scene, ruled by male bands with big hair, big swaggers, and a bombastic machismo, had long cried out for a feminist response, and it got one when a group of both casual and well-trained female musicians got together and called themselves the Chicago Women's Liberation Rock Band. The band was short-lived, lasting only from

1970 to 1973, but in that time they played more than one hundred gigs, combining their witty, off-kilter songs with apings of male rock-star posturing and thrilling audiences that often danced along in Rockette-style kick lines. Along with their East Coast counterpart, the New Haven Women's Liberation Rock Band, they released *Mountain Moving Day* in 1972. With songs such as "Sister Witch," "The Abortion Song," and "Papa Don't Lay That Shit on Me," and spoken-word pieces such as Naomi Weisstein's "Defending Yourself with Karate," the album was a document of the women's liberation movement with a backbeat.

Outside of movement anthems, the best thing to happen to women in music in the 1970s might have been the rise of the album-oriented radio format (AOR). Album-oriented radio allowed for radio stations to dispense with their former reliance on hit singles and instead play album tracks that weren't necessarily the catchiest or the most commercial. Record executives still concerned themselves with sniffing out hits, but the change in radio format brought blossoming success to a range of female artists—from soul stalwarts such as Gladys Knight and the Pips to singer-songwriters such as Carly Simon, Carole King, and Linda Ronstadt to showstoppers such as Cher. As the decade progressed, new genres (glam and glitter rock, funk, and punk) leaned heavily male but nevertheless produced genuine originals—the space-age funkstresses of LaBelle, the street-poet androgyne Patti Smith, and the all-female Filipino rockers Fanny.

There was still, of course, the question of combating an inbuilt sexism in both the structure of the music industry and its products. Rock gods the Rolling Stones had early on courted feminist ire with their hit "Under My Thumb"; in 1976, the band became Rock Enemy number 1 with the billboard ads for the album *Black and Blue*, which pictured a bruised, bound-up woman with the legend "I'm *Black and Blue* from the Rolling Stones—and I love it!" The group Women Against Violence Against Women (WAVAW) brought its outrage to Atlantic Records, the band's label, and the billboard was subsequently removed. But WAVAW's members would have their work cut out for them elsewhere in the industry, with album covers and song lyrics depicting women as bruised, lifeless, and/or animalistic playthings. (A 1977 *Time* magazine article called "Really Socking It to Women" mused on whether it was in spite of feminism or because of it that abusive images of women were everywhere. Advertising expert Jean Kilbourne weighed in thus: "Men are feeling guilty and sexually threatened. . . . The image of the abused woman is a logical extension of putting the uppity woman in her place.")

Elsewhere, the rock supergroupie had become a cultural icon in her own right. No longer a sweetly addled teen in the throes of Beatlemania, the groupie figure had grown to epic proportions. As rock tours became bigger and more theatrical, and as rock music itself came to signify a dangerous outlaw romance in which guitars were played like women, groupies were adopted as muses, mother figures, and, of course, sexual rewards for restless, road-weary musicians. Whether she was simply a girl willing to do almost anything for a backstage pass and a shot at her idol, or one of the more creative rock courtesans with a surefire band-grabbing gimmick (such as the Plaster Casters of Chicago, whose fearless leader Cynthia made plaster casts of the penises of lucky musicians), groupies had become as accepted a part of rock's status quo as leather pants and whiskey. And while this situation was great for girls who wanted to meet Led Zeppelin or Aerosmith and didn't mind kneeling down for the privilege, it was less so for a growing number of female rock writers, who often found themselves expected to put out to get their stories. *Life* magazine reporter Ellen Sander was assigned to cover Led Zeppelin's second U.S. tour, in 1969. After the final show at New York's Fillmore East, she entered the backstage area and was set upon by members of the band, who ripped off much of her clothing. She refused to complete the article.

But the man-equals-musician/girl-equals-groupie dynamic that had persisted in music was about to be broadened and complicated by a new medium. It was called MTV, and it transformed almost everything about the way music looked, sounded, and was understood.

You wouldn't know it now, but MTV used to stand for Music

Television. More to the point, it actually played music videos instead of an endless series of reality shows about young, dumb, and buff seekers of sex and fame. And most important, it literally changed the way television looked. Television narrative before MTV seemed to take place almost in real time—conversations were slow and evenly paced, plots moved sequentially from place to place. And the music videos that existed before 1981, the year MTV premiered, were simply brief performance films, often recorded at live concerts.

From the start, MTV pioneered a new style of television. Its videos cast musicians in minimovies, many of which were manic assemblages of quick cuts—a shot of the band playing, a shot of the band acting out a narrative, a shot of something random and symbolic, repeat. And right away, it changed the rules of success in the music industry. A memorable video could make a previously unremarkable musician into a tour-headlining star; likewise, bands that couldn't or wouldn't embrace the theatricality of MTV found their record sales outpaced by less talented but more videogenic groups.

From a feminist perspective, what was more important about MTV was that, for a short time, it presented a new and astounding picture of gender roles. By 1981, glam and glitter rock had offered up "heteroflexibility" and gender bending in the form of David Bowie, The New York Dolls, Patti Smith, and disco superstar Sylvester. But MTV made such imagery accessible to people—kids—who didn't have a front-row view at concert halls and nightclubs, giving over its heaviest rotations to boys who looked like girls and vice versa. There were Duran Duran, Rod Stewart, and Spandau Ballet with their long, frosted hair, elaborately draped scarves, tight pants, and pouty lips, and Prince and Adam Ant with their ruffled shirts and eyeliner. There were Grace Jones with her commanding height and flattop hairdo, Chrissie Hynde and Joan Jett in their leather pants, Annie Lennox in her natty suit and buzz-cut orange hair. The male and female gazes got all tangled up in videos such as Duran Duran's "Hungry Like the Wolf," in which a predatory, body-painted woman is identified in quick cuts, while shots of her prey—the fluffy-haired, pretty boys in the band—are lingering and sensual.

But though MTV became a showcase for innovative filmmaking and clever story lines, it also quickly fell back on the time-honored tactic of selling sex. Despite the fact that some of its most memorable early stars were women—Tina Turner, Pat Benatar, Dale Bozzio of Missing Persons, and Patty Smyth of Scandal, as well as the likes of Jones, Hynde, Jett, and Lennox—as the years passed MTV's women increasingly became more notable for their roles as backup dancers and sexual ornaments. They writhed in cages in Def Leppard videos, frolicked on beaches behind Huey Lewis and the News, and appeared as little more than cropped, oiled naughty parts in Duran Duran's "Girls on Film." (The video shown on MTV was a tamer version of the band's longer, soft-core porn film for the song, known euphemistically as the "European" cut.) Only a handful of years after the channel's birth, women's primary role on MTV seemed to have become that of hard-rock sex toy, scantily clad and wantonly posed behind guys with guitars—a role that began to parody itself with Robert Palmer's 1985 clip "Addicted to Love," in which an interchangeable band of miniskirted, scarlet-lipped fembots swiveled in unison behind the singer.

Still, a heady clutch of strong women persevered on MTV. And the format of the music video, with its rapid-fire imagery, narrative freedom, and pastiches of past and present, allowed these women (among them Tina Turner, Pat Benatar, and Madonna) and their videos to take on the male gaze in exciting, enduring ways. In the video for "Shadows of the Night," for instance, Benatar plays a 1940s-era Rosie the Riveter, who, in a moment of reverie, lays down her kerchiefed head and imagines that she's a daring spy leading a mission to blow up a Nazi headquarters. Security is breached, dynamite is planted, planes go down, and she's victorious—until, that is, she comes to and realizes, with a sigh of resignation, that she's still in the factory with her rivets. Even in the excitement of the jobs given to women during wartime, the video suggests, women still felt capable of much more. A few years later came Benatar's video for the song "Sex as a Weapon," which may still stand as the most explicit critique of the media ever seen on MTV. Benatar spends

© The Associated Press

Throughout her career, Madonna has used the tools of pop culture to reinvent herself again and again. She gained a wide audience in 1984 at the first annual MTV Music Video Awards ceremony, where she performed "Like a Virgin."

much of the video dancing in front of a bank of televisions whose screens flicker with image after image, juxtaposing *Playboy* bunnies, muscle men, and bikini models with images of her band playing along. At other times, the video is a pastiche: A 1950s image of a bottle of salad dressing or a can of furniture polish drops from the top of the frame, coming to rest on the bottom of an image of a pinup girl; a woman eats a hot dog suggestively as a clip-art illustration of a dominatrix wiggles alongside her.

But MTV's biggest star—maybe of all time—went further than any other woman in gleefully deploying the video format to shock, entrance, and manipulate viewers. With every new outing, Madonna donned a guise—winsome street urchin, hard-eyed peep-show dancer, Marilyn Monroe manqué, guilt-plagued Catholic girl, torch singer, shameless libertine—delighting and frustrating viewers who couldn't understand whether these personas were put-on or pretension or both. In her essay on race and representation called "Madonna: Plantation Mistress or Soul Sister?" bell hooks parses Madonna's appeal like so: "[W]hat some of us like about her is the way she deconstructs the myth of "natural" white girl beauty by exposing the extent to which it can be and is usually artificially constructed and maintained. She mocks the conventional racist defined beauty ideal even as she rigorously strives to embody it. . . . Madonna never lets her audience forget that whatever "look" she acquires is attained by hard work—it ain't natural."

Madonna's appeal to both women and gay men seemed obvious—though she wore that iconic "Boy Toy" belt buckle, she never appeared to be tamping down her overt sexuality for anyone. Even in videos such as "Borderline," in which she's playing a wannabe star done wrong by a playboy photographer, her confidence was palpable—she was the sex object who was actually the subject, and she never let the viewer forget it. Madonna also had a penchant for reinvention, a compelling creation myth of a working-class girl who scrapped her way to New York City and stardom, and she seemed obsessed with society's sexual mavericks and outsiders. Female fascination with Madonna even inspired a movie, *Desperately Seeking Susan*, in which the pop star played a lawless-yet-charming downtown scenester who upends the life of a lonely suburban wife. And Madonna particularly fascinated feminists: An entire gender- and cultural-studies curricula called Madonna Studies cropped up in the mid-1990s, with classes on Madonna's racial import, her Catholic iconography, her appropriation of queer subcultures, and more. Though other female singers would come to embody their decades' version of video stardom—Beyoncé Knowles, Britney Spears—it was the meeting of Madonna and MTV so early in their respective careers that made her what she was. And in the 1980s and '90s—decades which, for feminists, were filled with mixed cultural messages and a one-step-forward-two-steps-back sense of progress, Madonna's refusal to fess up to who and what she truly represented made her a logical, frustrating, and complex icon.

CHAPTER 4

WHAT WOMEN WANT: THE 1990S

IF FEMINISM'S RELATIONSHIP TO POPULAR culture had been uneasy since the dawn of the women's liberation movement, in the late 1980s and early 1990s it became downright hostile. Everywhere women turned, they were hit with indictments of women's gains: Magazine headlines purported to reveal "The Awful Truth About Women's Lib," newspapers suggested that feminism was responsible for everything from rising rates of divorce to a higher incidence of rape, and movies offered images of women driven by feminism and its byproducts to misery, loneliness, and murderous insanity.

The 1987 film *Fatal Attraction* set a new standard for feminist baiting in its story of a generally decent husband and father who is lured away from the bosom of his lovely family for a torrid affair with a single, liberated, working woman. The short result is mayhem. The longer story is that *Fatal Attraction* played out as a lurid cautionary tale pitting the independent, working woman against the traditional housewife. The housewife won, of course. Alex, the independent woman, so admirable and confident at first, was just below the surface a bundle of needs and disappointments. Sure, she was successful and had her own swanky loft and designer clothes, but what she really wanted, naturally, was her own man and family, and she would go to crazed, acid-flinging, bunny-boiling extremes to try to get it. In *Backlash: The Undeclared War Against American Women*, Susan Faludi recalls Adrian Lyne, the movie's director, giving his analysis of all the Alex-like women out there: "You hear feminists talk, and the last ten, twenty years you hear women talking about fucking men rather than being fucked, to be crass about it. It's kind of unattractive, however liberated and emancipated it is. It kind of fights the whole wife role, the whole childbearing role. Sure you got your career and your success, but you are not fulfilled as a woman."

What's most interesting about *Fatal Attraction*, as Faludi points out, is that its screenwriter, James Dearden, wrote it as a story about the consequences of a man's affair, a "moral tale about a man who transgresses and pays the penalty." Paramount Studios, which made the film, didn't want that gloss on the subject; it didn't want the man to take the fall or to come across as an unsympathetic character. Whatever the man had done, he had to be outvillained, and so the characters Dearden originally wrote were gradually made more extreme in script revisions—the man more moral, the woman more unhinged. To look at the movie knowing its backstory is to see the literal fear that independent women inspired. In the final, bloody showdown, Alex is killed and the nuclear family restored (minus the rabbit, of course); the subtext we're left with is that the single woman is such a threat to the status quo that she must literally be stopped in her tracks.

The Flawed TV Heroine

Working women on both the big and small screens spent the 1980s being scorned, humiliated, and punished for the dual sins of being ambitious and female. "Working women" at this time denoted not just the women who were infiltrating traditionally male realms of business, law, and other environs requiring a power suit, but also women who worked pink-collar factory, waitress, and secretarial jobs. And in 1988, one of them stood up and out in a big way. Her name was Roseanne Barr, and she managed not only to unseat TV's First Family—*The Cosby Show*'s Huxtables—but helped change how we all viewed the TV housewife/working mother.

Roseanne had been preceded by both put-upon matriarchs (such as Florida Evans on *Good Times*) and sassy working-class heroines (such as *Alice*'s title character, herself based on the character in the 1974 film *Alice Doesn't Live Here Anymore*). But she was the first to fuse both into a confrontational icon. Caustic, unsentimental, and overweight, with an oft-unemployed husband and three ingrate children, Roseanne and her family were the molecular opposites of the Huxtables. The *Cosby* clan was black, upwardly mobile, well groomed, and loving; the Connors were white, working class, slovenly, and antagonistic. Roseanne Connor was overworked and underappreciated: She had a factory job with a sexist boss, and when she got home she was responsible for the care and feeding of her kids and husband. She seemed physically incapable of emulating the TV housewife who makes it all seem sleek, effortless, and joyful; for Rosanne, both paid work and wifework were indistinguishable in their drudgery, and she had no interest in sugarcoating that for anyone. Roseanne embodied the frustration of what Arlie Hochschild called "the second shift": the situation faced by working women who, after a day at the factory or office, come home to continue working on the domestic front. In a 1987 *Ms.* article, sociologist Susan Dworkin called her a "symbol of the disgruntled American housewife, hanging in but perpetually pissed." And that was exactly how the real-life Roseanne Barr liked it: As she would later say of her character, "I never want her to be perfect. I want her to be flawed." But perhaps more important, she wanted her to not hide the reality of women everywhere in the very same boat.

Not everyone wanted to hear from such a proudly flawed character, though, and despite *Roseanne*'s unqualified success (the show was consistently high ranked throughout its nine seasons and won various Emmys and Golden Globes), Roseanne Barr herself had vocal, vicious, and, it will surprise no one to hear, largely male critics, who piled on with epithets such as "dog" and "bitch." Roseanne was loud, obnoxious, demanding, bawdy, and, of course, fat—in other words, she had all the unflattering characteristics ascribed to feminism itself. And furthermore, she wasn't playing a character: Roseanne Connor *was* Roseanne Barr, minus a few mitigating details, and Barr fought continually with the producers of the TV show to keep the character true to life.

Through the show's lifetime, Roseanne worked a series of jobs, all of which brought her into daily contact with both casual sexism and entrenched discrimination; one early story arc found her organizing a walkout at her manufacturing plant. But work itself didn't function as a signpost of Roseanne's feminism; as a working-class woman with a family, a job outside the home wasn't a choice—it was a necessity. But another sitcom that premiered in 1988, also created by a woman, did take women and work as its central theme, and it quickly became a barometer of shifting attitudes toward women, family, and workplace in the late 1980s and early '90s.

Murphy Brown, like *The Mary Tyler Moore Show* before it, was an ensemble comedy set in a media workplace; like *MTM*, its central character was a funny, attractive single woman. Murphy, unlike Mary, was never unsure of her right to be who or where she was in life; as a forty-year-old investigative reporter for a *60 Minutes*–like newsmagazine, Murphy wasn't only "allowed" to be pushy, stubborn, and often inappropriate, she was expected to be. And, like Roseanne Connor, she was shown as flawed from the start: In the pilot episode, Murphy (played by the tall, patrician Candice Bergen) has returned to the show, *FYI*, after a spin through the Betty Ford Clinic to address her alcoholism. As with *Roseanne*, the show was about lived feminism, and it modeled a workplace that, though invariably hectic and madcap, was more egalitarian that any other on TV at the time. It showed that women didn't have to compete with other women and could actually learn from one another: Murphy's Southern-belle coworker, Corky Sherwood, for instance, got regular doses of consciousness-raising from Murphy throughout the show's run. *Murphy Brown* also put forth the still-somewhat-radical idea that men and women could be colleagues and friends without sexual tension (or rank sexism) mucking everything up. And perhaps more important, it was one of the few shows on television during the 1980s that showed how a career could be a real source of satisfaction and pleasure for women.

But what *Murphy Brown* will always be remembered for is its inadvertent role in making "family values" the major political buzzword of the early 1990s. The story arc of the 1991–92 season of the show found Murphy making the decision to become a single mother; on the

When Murphy Brown chose to become a single mother, it set off a storm of criticism from the right wing, which attacked her for spurning "family values."

season's finale, she gave birth to son Avery as thirty-eight million viewers watched. Soon after, Vice President Dan Quayle made an example of Murphy in a speech to the Commonwealth Club of California; in decrying a "poverty of values" in the United States, Quayle chided, "[I]t doesn't help matters when prime-time TV has Murphy Brown—a character who supposedly epitomizes today's intelligent, highly paid, professional woman—mocking the importance of fathers, by bearing a child alone, and calling it just another 'lifestyle choice.'"

Quayle had already become something of a national joke by the time he called out Ms. Brown—he had, for instance, famously misspelled the word "potato" while judging a children's spelling bee—but nevertheless, his very public indictment of single mothers resonated quickly and loudly. Talk shows and news articles snapped up the story, offering a voice to Diane English, the show's creator and producer, and to real-life single mothers. And editorials in magazines such as *Time* rightly pointed out that if Quayle and his boss, George H. W. Bush, were truly concerned about "family values" and stemming a trend in single-parent households, perhaps they should look less to television and more to their own administration's views, such as the ones that opposed abortion and that penalized women on welfare for getting married.

It was clear that a substantial chunk of politicians and pop culture producers saw Working While Female as a problem that had to be managed. Television generally took a lighter hand than *Fatal Attraction*, with offerings such as the drama *The Days and Nights of Molly Dodd* (divorced working woman has nervous breakdown) and the sitcom *Who's the Boss?* (divorced working woman has no time for kids, hires fun father figure in the form of hunky manny). But in the end, the message was always the same: Single, working women are ticking time bombs of failure to be pitied rather than emulated. Faludi quotes the TV executive responsible for *Molly Dodd*: "'I think a lot of women ask themselves, What have we gotten out of [feminism]?' [Jay] Tarses says. 'Have we really gained anything? That's Molly Dodd's view.' If the show were to flash back on Molly in the early '70s, he says, viewers would meet a woman who 'probably would have pretended to be a radical feminist but secretly would have hoped for a more traditional life.' Why? 'Because that's how I feel about it,' Tarses says. 'I never did get what the women's movement was all about. . . . Every move a man made could be misconstrued by feminists.'"

And yet the ten-year period between 1985 and 1995 brought more female characters to television than ever before. In many cases, this happened via ensemble shows featuring more or less one-dimensional characters; the idea, perhaps, was that each woman acted as but one facet of what a real woman's personality might be. Take *The Golden Girls*, the unlikely hit sitcom about four sassy, elderly gals sharing a home in Florida and dealing with kids, dating, and sexuality and in the process showing a nation that women's lives didn't end with marriage, children, or menopause. On *Girls*, Bea Arthur played her character Dorothy as a version of her earlier

Maude—brash, ballbusting, and levelheaded. Her roommates were Rose (the sweet, dumb one), Blanche (the shallow, slutty one), and Sophia (the obnoxious, conniving one—who also happened to be Dorothy's mother). The four-adds-up-to-one formula was repeated on other sitcoms: *Living Single*'s quartet of black career woman included Khadija (the driven, practical magazine editor), Synclaire (the sweet and dumb cousin), Regine (their shallow and slutty roommate), and Max (Khadija's obnoxious, conniving lawyer pal). Dramas put a slightly different spin on the formula, with shows such as *thirtysomething* and *Sisters* using their quartets of female characters to illustrate the imagined life paths of a certain class of woman: Working motherhood? Happy homemaking? All-career-all-the-time? Irresponsible hedonism? Every one of these shows, however, tendered an implied judgment on each woman, a silent accounting of how she spent her time, whether she was a good enough wife and mother, and whether she deserved to be loved.

That said, there were also more lighthearted female-centric shows on prime time: the windswept historical drama *Dr. Quinn, Medicine Woman*, the bawdy fashionista send-up *Veronica's Closet*, and even the good-natured *Ellen*, whose famous 1997 coming-out episode—in which the fictional Ellen, played by real-life lesbian Ellen DeGeneres, admits she's gay—was shocking only because of how long it took to get there. And there were increasing numbers of female leads on "procedural" dramas such as *ER* and *Law & Order* in which both women and men prosecuted crimes, performed surgeries, and—in the case of *The X Files*—tracked aliens. But it wasn't until the end of the 1990s that a female TV character engendered as much controversy, confusion, and feminist theory as Roseanne and Murphy Brown had a decade earlier.

Her name was Ally McBeal, and she looked to be a literal lightweight, lacking both the physical bulk of Roseanne and the assured mien of Murphy. When *Ally McBeal*, the show, made its debut in 1997, it was clear that Ally McBeal, the character, was designed to appeal to what was increasingly considered to be a television audience uninterested

Girls Kick Ass! (Er, Not You, Lara Croft.)

One of girl power's handiest all-purpose slogans, "Girls Kick Ass," started out as the humble tagline for a line of girly skateboard-culture clothing called Poot! But the term got literal with a slew of TV series, books, and cartoons that came to dominate 1990s pop culture. Though Lara Croft, the impossibly buxom heroine of the *Tomb Raider* video games, was by the late '90s the most mainstream pretender to a girls-kick-ass throne, she was also the pixilated embodiment of a male gaze–centric fantasy of what a heroic woman looked like. But there were more—and better—contenders out there. Here's a brief survey of some of the best.

Xena: Warrior Princess, 1995–2001
The character Xena first reared her majestic head in several episodes of *Hercules: The Legendary Journeys.* On *Hercules,* Xena was a warlord and a villain; on her own spinoff, she was a conflicted heroine—her warmongering days were behind her, but she was regularly tasked with fighting adversaries both human and supernatural in plotlines that borrowed liberally from Greek mythology and Homeric epics. Perhaps more important, she looked good in her breastplates and battle gear and titillated a generation of girls with a heavy-on-the-subtext friendship with her loyal sidekick Gabrielle.

Buffy the Vampire Slayer, 1997–2003
The movie that inspired this cult TV series was nothing to write home about; the story of a vapid cheerleader who finds out she's been chosen by fate as a "slayer" who must do eternal battle with vampires, demons, and sundry other baddies, it was a campy, lightweight outing. The TV series, however, was something different: Series creator Joss Whedon offered a witty, philosophical look at what happens when high school, so often referred to as hell, turns out to literally be just that. Buffy herself was the horror-movie trope of the victimized blond turned on its head—a vision of unlikely strength and heroism who, weirdly enough, became more human as the world around her got increasingly supernatural. But even fans of the show wondered about its ultimate message; it was tempting to question whether *Buffy*, like *Xena*, posited that the strongest heroines exist only in the realm of the fantastic.

The Powerpuff Girls, 1998–2005
Once upon a time, a mad scientist fused sugar, spice, and everything nice—as well as a dash of Chemical X—and came up with the fiercest trio of five-year-old crime fighters since . . . well, ever. Blossom, Bubbles, and Buttercup were the saucer-eyed trio of the title; the tots defended their city, Townsville, from such menaces as robbers and aliens, but they found plenty of time to deal with kindergarten-type problems such as how to live without a security blanket. Though it seems overanalytical to call the Powerpuff Girls agents of third-wave feminism, they did put a sweetly subversive spin on girl power—and it didn't hurt that their father figure was nurturing, hovering, and more like a den mother than a mad scientist.

Sailor Moon, 1992–1997
This media megafranchise encompassed manga, anime, and video games, but its central story was that of an ordinary Japanese schoolgirl who, like Buffy, discovers that there's more to her than she originally thought—namely, an ability to transform into a magical superhero imbued with the power of the solar system. Along with a crew of teen girls, Sailor Moon must lead the charge to defend the earth from the apocalyptic Dark Kingdom. Sailor Moon and her pals were both less violent and more earnest than the Powerpuff Girls, but on reaching American shores in the late '90s, they were promptly welcomed into the girl-power fold.

Fearless, 1999–2004
Prolific young-adult author Francine Pascal was perhaps best known for creating the soapy, stereotype-laden book series *Sweet Valley High* during the 1980s; the series *Fearless* was her gritty entry into the girl-power stakes. The books told the story of Gaia, a New York City teen who was born without the "fear gene." With some anger issues to work out—her father, a CIA operative, disappeared when her mother was murdered— Gaia prowls the seamy edges of town, looking for trouble, and more often than not finds it. *Fearless* was fascinating because, unlike female heroines who won't kick ass until provoked, Gaia was proactive in her fury and willing to get knocked around in the process—a female vigilante who broke the mold.

in the usual tropes of feminism. Ally was a young lawyer who was reminiscent of Mary Richards with her spunky, comic insecurities, but who was ostensibly thoroughly modern in her priorities in life and love. This was a character who made it clear where she stood on feminism with the statement, "I plan to change [society.] But I'd just like to get married first."

And indeed, Ally proved not to be a feminist character. Yes, she was a young woman who, we were to understand, grew up seeing the changes feminism had forged in the world. Feminism had empowered her to go to law school; feminism made it possible for her to identify what was and was not appropriate behavior from her male colleagues. But since she turned every minute of her workday into an opportunity for narcissistic self-reflection and spent the rest of her time either falling down or blowing up, it was hard to feel sisterly toward her.

And the show's plotlines used every opportunity to take cheap and mean-spirited shots at feminism and female capability in the form of court cases that touched on hot-potato issues such as breast-augmentation surgery, hostile-work-environment sexual-harassment cases, and self-defense—most of which ended up pressing the conclusion that all such cases were malicious (and ultimately dismissible) vendettas against men by women who couldn't handle their own lives. (Ally's smarmy boss served as the show's official mouthpiece for statements suggesting that all this women's rights stuff had gone too far: In one episode, he argued that women should qualify under the Federal Disabilities Act because "they cannot contend with having to do a job and have a man smile at them.") During its five-season run, the show consistently avoided taking responsibility for its statements, preferring instead to dress them up in slapstick humor and fantasy sequences; the result was a show that was as intoxicated with its own cleverness as it was terrified that someone—a woman, no doubt—might actually take it seriously.

But *Ally McBeal* quickly became a cultural flashpoint, and articles and news stories ran fast and thick through the mainstream media. "Ally McBeal: Woman of the '90s or Retro Airhead?" wondered one headline, while another queried, "Is Ally McBeal a Nineties Heroine? Or a Grotesque Creation of Male Fantasy?" Reporters questioned real-life female lawyers to find out if Ally's micro–mini skirt suits, or her firm's co-ed bathroom, would fly in actual legal firms. Again, the mainstream media were using fictional characters as stand-ins for real women, and Ally was a perfect straw woman: She was irritating enough to knock down but conflicted enough to be held up as "proof" that women didn't really want feminism—they just, in the end, wanted to be loved and validated.

Ally was the American answer to Bridget Jones, the British heroine of the trans-Atlantic bestseller *Bridget Jones's Diary*, which followed a young, single book publicist as she obsessed over her weight and bumbled through a series of hetero romantic disasters. Bridget herself was the most visible icon of what was coming to be known as "chick lit"—fiction written by young, single working women about young, single working women, in which struggles with identity and feminism were paid lip service, but in which the plot still centered on finding a man, getting married, and achieving the real reward of societal approval. Essayist Daphne Merkin, writing in a 1998 issue of *The New Yorker*, posited that Bridget and Ally elicited such strong reactions from feminist women because they boldly represented the underbelly that those feminists were ashamed to reveal: "If Gloria Steinem had told us the whole truth . . . she might have sounded like Bridget Jones. God knows, both women worry about the size of their thighs, though only one of them has gone public with that undignified anxiety."

Whether or not you believed Merkin that Steinem, like Bridget, went home every night to measure the circumference of her thighs and record it in her diary, the gauntlet had been thrown down: Feminists hated Bridget and Ally, apparently, because we hated our own weaknesses and our inability to model the perfect, conflict- and regret-free feminist existence. Furthermore, we were told, we hated them because we didn't want to admit that maybe feminism wasn't enough, and that we wanted love and a perfectly toned butt perhaps more than we wanted equal rights. Author Helen Fielding herself suggested that

Bridget Jones's Diary functioned as a sort of get-out-of-feminist-jail-free card, noting in a 1998 *Harper's Bazaar* profile, "It might come as a relief to American women that this is a book about being as crap as everyone is. . . . Maybe it's okay not to be a superwoman."

If the hairy-legged women's libber had been the dominant media image of a feminist in the 1970s, and the power-suited working woman the symbol of the '80s, the Ally McBeal/Bridget Jones duo served as the icon of the '90s, though both women came along in the decade's last few years. And what are icons if not marketing tools? Soon enough, the media and pop culture landscape was flooded with Ally and Bridget knockoffs and look-alikes. Though women in general seemed to be flourishing in the 1990s—owning their own businesses in record numbers, matching men in college admissions and earning potential, and becoming increasingly visible in art and politics—the default image of women quickly became that of the Allyesque, Bridget-like single striver. And a new quartet of pop culture women was about to be added to the mix.

Sex and the City started as a newspaper column by New York girl-about-town Candace Bushnell in 1994, was published as a book three years later, and was revamped in its most famous guise, an HBO series, in 1998. "SATC," the column, was credited with providing the literary pole for what became Bridget and Ally's cheerily neurotic single-girl flag waving, but though the TV show shared similarities with the chick-lit genre, its form of spinster-baiting was actually secondary to its celebration of single women's economic independence.

As with the women on *The Golden Girls* and *Living Single* before it, *SATC*'s characters were each painted as the embodiment of an urban female stereotype: the one who sleeps around, the one who's bitter and lonely, the one who's romantic, and the one who can't stop questioning it all. And as on those shows—and perhaps more important, unlike Bridget and Ally—the characters had little interest in whining about their personal deficiencies and depended on each other, rather than on lovers, for their emotional satisfaction. As Bushnell wrote in the book, "We were hard and proud of it, and it hadn't been easy to get to this point—this place of complete independence, where we had the luxury of treating men like sex objects. It had taken hard work, loneliness, and the realization that, since there might never be anyone there for you, you had to take care of yourself in every sense of the word."

This was not, on its face, so different a concept from what many second-wave feminists had advocated. Depending on someone else for money, for a roof over your head, or for emotional fulfillment was illogical, and though earlier pop culture products had tacitly acknowledged this, *SATC* made it explicit—and, for good measure, illustrated that the larger world wasn't quite ready for such a radical concept. (An early episode of the TV show found successful lawyer Miranda buying an apartment and at every turn bumping up against disbelief that she was actually doing so by herself, no husband, no father.) *Sex and the City*, with its premise that women in their thirties who have enough money and power don't need men for anything but sex, seemed to reduce all the goals of feminism to one: cold, hard cash. This idea was echoed elsewhere in popular culture, where top-selling female groups such as Destiny's Child sang about a feminism that was all about the Benjamins, and the net worth of women such as Oprah Winfrey and Julia Roberts was emblazoned on magazine covers as shorthand for their power.

To *Sex and the City*'s credit, its plots did acknowledge that equating money with liberation was a simplistic conclusion. In one early episode, for instance, the women argue over how Carrie should feel about the fact that a man she'd slept with gave her a handful of cash the next day. "What're you getting so uptight about?" asked Samantha. "I mean, money is power. Sex is power. Therefore, getting money for sex is simply an exchange of power." "Don't listen to the dime-store Camille Paglia," was Miranda's response. Though the exchange didn't go much further, like many subsequent plotlines on the show it put forth the understanding that a feminism based only in economics overshadowed more crucial philosophical aspects of women's struggle for equality.

"If You Let Me Play": Selling to Women with the Language of Empowerment

If you spent any time watching TV or reading newspapers or magazines before the 1990s, you knew quite well that the basic rules of advertising were as rigid as they'd been for decades, depending on conventional wisdom of how households looked (two heterosexual parents, several kids, a pet) and how their labor was divided. Cars, tools, and electronics were marketed to men. Everything else—floor polish, toothpaste, diapers, instant rice, air freshener—was marketed to women. Beginning in the 1990s, however, it seemed that advertisers were actually trying to broaden their conceptions of what consumers looked like.

Before we start thinking that advertising got progressive, however, it's important to understand how an industrywide sea change originating in television affected advertising. The TV-biz process of "narrowcasting"—targeting a carefully selected audience demographic—became more crucial than ever before in the 1990s, because there were simply more channels from which viewers could choose. Where once there had been only ABC, NBC, and CBS, the big three were joined during the decade by youth-hungry "baby nets" such as the WB, UPN, and FOX, to say nothing of a growing number of cable channels, some of which, such as Oxygen, Lifetime, and WE (Women's Entertainment), were explicitly aimed at a female audience. So narrowcasting was the obvious route to making sure advertisers got the viewers they wanted for their products. Needless to say, advertising started to get very, very specific.

Take the new "badass" category, which advertised things to women that had traditionally been the domain of men, and which did so by appropriating impressionistic bits of women's movement language. When Mountain Dew rebranded itself in the mid-'90s as the beverage of choice for "extreme" athletes, the gonzo mountain bikers, bungee jumpers, and snowboarders featured in its commercials were always young men. But the company threw a bone to the ladies with a 1997 commercial set to a revved-up rendition of Maurice Chevalier's eminently creepy classic, "Thank Heaven for Little Girls." Sung by snarling British punk Lesley Rankine and her band Ruby, the lyrics

"Thank heaven for little girls/For little girls get bigger every day" were intercut with footage of sweat-soaked women yelling as they soared, crashed, and swung across the screen. Likewise, Lady Foot Locker deployed an ad for running shoes that featured a sludgy, rocking rework of Helen Reddy's "I Am Woman."

In a more sentimental take, Nike's 1995 campaign titled "If You Let Me Play" featured a multiracial montage of little girls speaking directly to the viewer about the advantages that come from participating in sports. "If you let me play sports," one said plaintively, "I will like myself more." "I will have more self-confidence," added another. The benefits went on: "I'll be 50 percent less likely to get breast cancer. . . . I will suffer less depression. . . . I will be more likely to leave a man who beats me. . . . I'll be less likely to be pregnant before I want to. . . . I will learn to be strong." The Nike ad indirectly referenced Title IX of the Education Amendments Act passed in 1972, which stated that girls and women could not be denied participation in any sports program receiving federal funding; though girls' participation in sports indeed grew exponentially once Title IX was passed, by the mid-1990s, it still had plenty of opposition from high schools and colleges that complained that a focus on girls' sports would take away from boys'.

As the 1990s turned into the 2000s, companies got increasingly shameless in appropriating the language of liberation to sell stuff to women and girls. In 1999, an ad for Barbie featured not the statuesque plastic sweetheart herself but instead a real girl grasping a hockey stick, with a tagline that read simply "Become Your Own Hero." Virginia Slims' erstwhile "You've Come a Long Way, Baby" was tweaked in the mid-'90s to become "It's a woman thing"; the slogan changed again toward the end of the decade as the brand began to target a more multicultural demographic, and the resulting "Find your voice" campaign once again used smoking to illustrate women's freedom, empowerment, and entitlement to kill themselves as effectively as men. The most egregious offenders turned up in 2003 and 2004: One, an almost incomprehensible campaign for Barely There lingerie, tried to convince us that if Betsy Ross had been invited to sign the Declaration of Independence, her main concern would have been doing so in underwear that didn't ride up her bum. The other advertised Lean Cuisine's frozen diet pizza by suggesting it was a landmark for women on par with the right to vote.

Another spin on liberation, ad-style, came in the form of shills for spendy products that assured women that their independence and freedom were a wonderful reason to buy things. De Beers, the company that invented both the tradition of the diamond engagement ring and the catchphrase that's sold millions of them ("A diamond is forever"), saw a potential new market in status-conscious, financially solvent '90s women, and it immediately started offering them trinkets that "celebrated" their independence. A 1999 print ad for its diamond solitaire necklace featured a woman, her face half in shadow, with the words, "It beckons me as I pass the store window. A flash of light in the corner of my eye. I stop. I turn. We look at each other. And though I'm not usually that kind of girl, I take it home."

The message was clear: This was no demure bride-to-be accepting her fiancé's bent-knee proposal with downcast eyes and a teary smile; this was a coy, self-assured hussy who didn't need a man to buy her diamonds, and that made her "that kind of girl." A few years later, the company went further, suggesting that wearing a diamond ring on the right hand, rather than the left, was a feminist statement. De Beers's line of right-hand rings featured diamonds in non-nuptial shapes and settings and was designed to, in the company's words, symbolize "the strength, success, and independence of women of the twenty-first century." The subtext of the ad, however, was equally clear: Advertisers would not stop looking for ways to make women buy things they didn't need just because those women weren't looking for men and marriage. Rather, the sales pitch would just have to get craftier, validating single women and urging them to "reward" their own independence with products.

A 1999 ad for Coca-Cola featured an illustration of a confident woman, blueprints tucked under her arm, with the legend, "When you make your own choices, go for what's real." And even breast implant manufacturers got in on the act: One ad for Mentor breast implants featured a close-up of a smiling young women and the introduction, "Amber O'Brien, 25, is having the time of her life. Recently, she decided it was time to have breast augmentation." It was an example of consumer feminism at its finest—by going on to list all the ways in which Amber was solvent and successful, the ad recast risky and expensive cosmetic surgery as something one did for its own sake. The logic of this ad—the logic of the idea of consumer feminism in general—went like this: You want a diamond necklace/can of Coke/breast implants, and you're a single, successful woman who can afford them. So you get them, because why should you have to wait for a man to buy you a diamond/a fizzy beverage/new breasts? Buying these things yourself is a statement of your independence. So even though the engine behind these products is questionable—the civil war and human-rights atrocities endemic to the diamond trade in Africa, the health risks of breast implants, the monolithic beauty industry that to thrive depends on perpetuating a cycle of women's insecurity—it's your choice, so it must be empowering. Right?

How Riot Grrrl Became Girl Power

Though the larger culture seemed sure it had figured out what women wanted from their lives romantically, economically, and materially, the music industry was a locus of questioning, a state of affairs that made for a short but unquestionably fertile time when music was a chief site of feminism and mainstream resistance. Some of the most powerful music made by women in the 1990s was, in a word, reactive. Men dominated both mainstream and underground music, and the female voices chafing against that fact seemed amplified. The rapper Queen Latifah took on sexism in hip-hop with the anthemic "U.N.I.T.Y," in which she asked men, "Who you callin' a bitch?," while her fellow rappers Salt-N-Pepa released hit after hit agitating for women's sexual agency and pleasure against insanely catchy beats—among them "Let's Talk About Sex," "None of Your Business," and "Shoop." A young New Yorker named Ani DiFranco was self-distributing cassette tapes of low-fi, high-intellect songs about battling street harassment, embracing sisterhood, and negotiating sexual desire in a sexist world. And a loose coalition of young women, disillusioned by the male-dominated punk scene, were about to introduce the world to a concept called Riot Grrrl.

Riot Grrrl was a direct descendant of the radical feminism of the late 1960s and early 1970s, born of consciousness-raising and raw anger at how girls were sidelined by the punk music they truly loved: It was untrained, ugly, and authentic. The scene—with its most vocal outposts in Washington, DC, and Olympia, Washington, as well as London—was a patchwork of rap sessions, homemade zines with titles such as *Girl Germs* and *Bikini Kill*, garage bands, and guerrilla theater. Riot grrrls wrote about personal issues—among them rape and sexual abuse by family members—and raged about loving punk music but hating the guys who thought girls didn't belong in mosh pits. They called out punk boys for their complicity in perpetuating sexism and scrawled SLUT and WHORE on their own stomachs as an acknowledgment of society's limited vision of women who refuse to conform. They also embraced the power of girlhood, of seizing the moment before "anything is possible" becomes "everything is circumscribed." Rachel Fudge writes of this confrontational approach in her essay "Girl, Unreconstructed: Why Girl Power Is Bad for Feminism":

> *Those extra rs in riot grrrl weren't just wacky wordplay: They quite literally put the* grrr *into being a girl. . . . The cries for revolution woven through the lyrics, slogans, and zines were in part a youthful flirtation with extreme rhetoric, but riot grrrls were also dead serious about changing the world, starting with the circumstances of their own lives. When the U.K. band Huggy Bear sang 'Boredom, rage, fierce intention, this is the sound of revolution . . .' over grinding, spiraling ill-tuned guitars and manic, out-of-sync drums, it did sound like a revolution was right around the corner.*

Many riot grrrls had seen the female musicians of their youths, such as the Go-Gos, run through a sort of music-industry wash cycle in which the music had all the subversion and discomfort wrung out of it until it was bland, sellable, and willing to pose in its underwear on the cover of *Rolling Stone*. This movement wanted no part of that, and so the women and girls involved did everything themselves, from making the zines to promoting the shows to putting together conferences. And as media started sniffing around the scene, its members sought to strictly control their coverage, rightly concerned that their message could too easily be distorted and used against them. The little coverage they sanctioned came from teen magazine *Sassy*, an early champion of Riot Grrrl that enthusiastically plugged its music, zines, and ideas in its pages throughout the movement's lifespan.

Unfortunately, riot grrrls' refusal to talk to mainstream media gave such media free rein to weave overblown, wildly off-base characterizations of the movement. *Newsweek* asserted that "Riot Girl [*sic*] is feminism with a loud happy face dotting the 'i'"; Britain's *Mail on Sunday* warned its readers that "Every word [riot grrrls] scream is a prayer against men. . . . They call themselves feminists but theirs is a feminism of rage and, even, fear." Without the actual voices of riot grrrls to depend on, the press managed in record time to reduce the rhetoric and the goals of the movement to some fearmongering sound bites and peppy fashion statements. And in the ultimate irony, it wasn't long before the riot grrrls' raw emotion and conscious rejection of the mainstream was candy-coated and repackaged by a British singing group known as the Spice Girls.

The utterly contrived quintet was assembled by the impresario Simon Fuller (who later went on to create the pop culture landmark *American Idol*), who gave each Spice Girl a flavor—Sporty, Baby, Scary, Ginger, and Posh—a trademark look (each of which involved push-up bras and hot pants), and an easily digestible raison d'être known as "girl power." What was this girl power? It wasn't quite clear, and the Spice Girls themselves didn't seem to know either. Their biggest hit, "Wannabe," offered to tell the listener "What I really, really want," which was, apparently, to "Zig-a-zig-hah." The Spice Girls' official guide, *Girl Power!*, dispensed such gems as "I expect an equal relationship where he does as much washing

The Sassiest Magazine in America

It's hard not to talk about *Sassy* without getting a little, well, girl-powery. For young women who were actually teenagers when the magazine made its debut, it was a bona fide revelation. Teen magazines had for years urged conformity of their female readers, advertised engagement rings and hope chests alongside fashion spreads, and talked about sex only in terms of "don't do it." *Sassy* changed all that. It had frank stories about real teenagers—from skinheads to lesbians to political activists and beyond. It had headlines such as "13 Reasons to Stop Dieting" and "A Day in the Life of Miss America, Indentured Servant." Its fashion spreads urged girls to shop vintage, make their own clothes, and dress like Bob Dylan and Audrey Hepburn. It tipped the sacred cows of teen culture, writing that prom night "sucks" and calling out then-hot icons such as New Kids on the Block and Tiffani-Amber Thiessen for being, respectively, manufactured schlock and a "demi-bimbo." And it had writers who talked to—not talked down to—the magazine's readers.

When *Sassy* launched in 1988, its publisher, Australian entrepreneur Sandra Yates, had a very specific idea in mind. Yates didn't understand why American teen magazines were, in her words, "like *Good Housekeeping* for teenagers, speaking with parental voices and suspended in aspic," and she wanted to create something that spoke to teen girls in their own voice. She

up as I do" but offered little interrogation of the bedrock reasons why those inequities needed adjusting in the first place (to say nothing of questioning why "he" was automatically the partner in question).

Given the mainstream press's long-standing disdain for anything overtly feminist, it was sadly logical that the Spice Girls came to stand in for explicitly feminist analysis. (As journalist Jennifer Pozner pointed out ruefully in a 1998 *Sojourner* article, "It's probably a fair assumption to say that 'zizazig-ha' is not Spice shorthand for 'subvert the dominant paradigm.'") And unlike Riot Grrrl, Girl Power had something both marketers and consumers wanted. Girl power could sell. And so it was promptly run through the retail cogs, emerging on the other end as a series of flashy consumables: knee socks, barrettes, hair dye, nail polish, and more, all packaged in "subversive" colors and peppy patterns. There modeled *Sassy* on Australia's *Dolly* magazine and staffed it with editors and writers who were in many cases only a few years out of their teens. *Sassy* reflected a real culture of girls in part because it was created by those girls: They wrote in with their problems and true stories for regular features such as "Zits and Stuff" and "It Happened to Me"; their style savvy was highlighted in regular girl-on-the-street fashion features and contests such as "Sassiest Girl in America," and their voices came through in the magazine's features on everything from Ireland's civil war to gay siblings to girl geeks.

Not everyone was so thrilled about a teen magazine that aimed for more than selling maxipads and mascara. During its eight-year lifespan, *Sassy*'s frank talk on such daring topics as masturbation and alternative sexualities led to numerous boycotts, sponsor pullouts, and letter-writing campaigns by so-called family values coalitions. In the end, it was these struggles that brought down the magazine, leaving both editors and readers frustrated and heartbroken.

More than a decade after its demise, *Sassy* might be more popular in retrospect than it was while on newsstands. There's a bevy of writing celebrating the magazine—including a behind-the-scenes book called *How Sassy Changed My Life*—and back issues sell briskly on eBay. The magazine is widely credited for its prescience in championing everything from Riot Grrrl to baby T-shirts. And even though it was an aberration, many of us still hold out hope that someday, something like it can exist again.

was a girl-power mall store (Hot Topic), a girl-power movie (the Spice Girls' own *Spice World*), and even a girl-power campaign launched by the U.S. Department of Health and Human Services, whose vaguely stated goal was to "help encourage and motivate 9- to 13-year-old girls to make the most of their lives."

The embrace of "girl power" as a concept wasn't, in theory, a negative thing. Academics and psychologists who studied girlhood had previously noted that it was a time in many women's lives that was particularly powerful, writing that prepubescent females often believed in themselves and their potential much more than adolescent girls and young women. Lyn Mikel Brown and Carol Gilligan's landmark 1992 book *Meeting at the Crossroads* revealed that girls' self-esteem tends to plummet once they hit puberty and are surrounded by prescriptive pop culture messages of what it means to be female. However, the way that "girlie" and "girl power" were adopted as shorthand for a kind of diet feminism that substituted consumer trappings for actual analysis was limiting, to put it mildly.

Still, at the same time the media were falling over themselves to identify girl icons and co-opt grrrl anger, there were heartfelt attempts to redefine women's music away from easy labels. One of these was the Lilith Fair, organized in 1997 by Canadian musician Sarah McLachlan. McLachlan and coconspirators such as Paula Cole had become increasingly frustrated by the ongoing secondary status of female musicians on concert bills and radio stations. The conventional wisdom was that male artists were the bread and butter of the mainstream; radio programmers and concert promoters freely admitted that they wouldn't play two female artists back to back or book more than one or two female artists on a festival roster. The Lilith Fair was another example of women elbowing their way into a space despite being told it couldn't be done. And the 1997 tour turned out to be the top-grossing festival tour of the year—no small feat with such testosterone-pumped competitors as the Warped Tour, Ozzfest, and Lollapalooza.

The Lilith Fair wasn't the first all-female music festival, of course. The long-running Michigan Womyn's Music Festival—at which women are not only 100 percent of the performers but also build, staff, promote, and manage the entire weeklong event—had been around since 1976; along with other women's music festivals, it was considered a crucial feature of the largely lesbian-identified "women's music" genre. Like the disgruntled music fans and musicians behind the Chicago and New Haven Women's Liberation Rock Bands of the 1970s, the women who became the key voices in women's music—including Cris Williamson, Holly Near, and Sweet Honey in the Rock—were profoundly tired of seeing talented female performers shunted to the sidelines of a mainstream music scene in which the most acceptable role for a women was still that of backup singer or groupie. By creating a separate space for women to make music outside the mainstream— with their own concerts, record labels, producers, and distribution channels—these women made female voices their priority in a very literal way.

Women's music was also keenly political, with a focus on lesbian identity and lesbian separatism, which reasoned that existing, ingrained power dynamics between men and women made heterosexual relationships politically impossible and advocated lesbianism as the key to living feminism. Though some musicians crossed over to *Billboard*-style pop recognition—among them Tracy Chapman and the Indigo Girls—much of the lyrical and political content of women's music was simply too controversial for a mainstream audience.

The Lilith Fair served as a kind of bridge between women's music and the mainstream. It was more commercial than festivals such as Michigan—unapologetically commercial, in fact, with corporate sponsors from the prosaic (Starbucks) to the irritatingly gender-specific (Bioré, whose reps distributed enough blackhead-removing strips at the festival's stops to keep an entire nation blemish-free)—but it also donated a percentage of each stop's profits to local and national nonprofits across the United States and Canada, including Planned Parenthood, the Breast Cancer Fund, and the Rape, Abuse, and Incest National Network (RAINN). The tour was also safely unchauvinist: Though conservative naysayers such as Jerry Falwell were quick to speak out against the festival as promoting paganism and lesbianism, plenty of men were involved in staffing and promotion as well as in the bands themselves (in many acts, from Paula Cole to Jewel, the men in the backing bands far outnumbered the women on stage).

However, for those who had hoped that an all-women's festival could be as radical in execution as it seemed in theory, Lilith couldn't help but seem like a bit of a step back. This was in part because, with the array of strong, edgy women performers who had come up in the early- to mid-1990s, the roster of artists on the Lilith stage seemed to lack a certain . . . well, *grrr.* Sarah MacLachlan's ethereal stage presence and soaring ballads were beautiful, sure, but they didn't exactly foment a revolution. And though Paula Cole's hit "Where Have All the

Cowboys Gone?" was, according to the singer, written with tongue firmly in cheek, it sounded so . . . well, sincere. Though by this time in the 1990s, we had heard Liz Phair sing her strong-girl-wronged songs and listened to the raw, dissonant outrage of frontwomen such as the Gits' Mia Zapata, Hole's Courtney Love, and Sonic Youth's Kim Gordon, few artists who didn't conform to a traditionally "feminine" form of musicianship and stage presence appeared on the tour. The question of whether Lilith Fair would be a self-constructed musical ghetto was worth pondering as well. After all, if Lilith's male-dominated counterparts such as Lollapalooza and Ozzfest didn't invite more women to take part because they assumed those women would be part of "the chick festival," but those same women were excluded from Lilith, it wasn't exactly a blow for inclusion. Further complicating things was the suddenly rampant problem of sexual threats and abuse at big music festivals. Did creating a "safe space" at a festival such as Lilith mean that the onus was no longer on unisex festivals to make sure that their participants behaved decently? (It was a question that seemed particularly salient in the summer of 1999, when reports from the dude-heavy festival Woodstock '99 included stories of rape in the mosh pits and attacks on female festivalgoers by male security personnel.)

In the end, Lilith was short-lived; the festival ceased after the summer of 1999, and subsequent all-women festival lineups seemed to return to a pre–Girl Power format of smaller, anticorporate, and do-it-yourself events, the most prominent of which were known as Ladyfest. Ladyfest, like Riot Grrrl, began in the do-it-yourself college town of Olympia, Washington, in 2000, offering shows, workshops, and art with a feminist bent; proceeds were donated to nonprofits, and the event was an all-volunteer affair. The idea spread rapidly, and within just a few years, Ladyfests had blossomed in cities all over the world, each independently run but always with a female focus and a grounding in feminist DIY principles.

But in the realm of the mainstream, the end of Lilith Fair left a noticeable hole. Conspiracy theorists will note that in the mainstream arena, music took a decidedly macho tone for several years after the ascent of both the Spice Girls and the Lilith Fair; the rise of a hypermasculine rock-rap hybrid called "nu metal," typified by Limp Bizkit and Korn, seemed in direct opposition to Lilith's sisterly softness, and the puerile, boys-only antics of bands such as Blink-182 hit the mainstream with full force as Lilith's run wound down. And though "girl power" continued to be used as a marketing buzzword for everything from Barbies to frozen yogurt, the feminism that was originally behind its battle cry was receding further and further into the background of pop culture.

"Is Feminism Dead?"

Since the early 1990s, the term "third wave" had become entrenched in discussions of feminism, but it proved to be a difficult concept to pin down. Like an ideological lump of clay, the descriptor was passed through the hands of both individuals and collectives who molded it according to their needs and desires: For one person, "third wave" might denote a feminism that was less about collective action than about individual choices; for another, it was a feminism that sought to incorporate and prioritize a slew of issues and identities marginalized by previous waves—women of color, working-class women, transgender folks.

These varied definitions resulted in part from the fact that third wave theory, in a formal sense, was far less structured than the feminist theory that had come before. The texts published in the early to mid-1990s that became synonymous with third wave feminism didn't offer "aha!" moments such as Adrienne Rich's "compulsory heterosexuality" or Betty Friedan's "problem with no name." Rather, anthologies such as Rebecca Walker's *To Be Real: Telling the Truth and Changing the Face of Feminism* and Barbara Findlen's *Listen Up: Voices from the Next Feminist Generation* focused on stories of individual identity and struggle. The writers in these anthologies sought to reconcile what each of them knew about feminism with the realities of life as a biracial woman, or an anorexic, or a hip-hop fan. Here was a catchphrase of the second

"A Little Touch of Ladies First": Women and Hip-Hop

In the feminist politics of entertainment, women and hip-hop have enjoyed a relationship that's been as fruitful as it has been antagonistic. The first ladies of the hip-hop era were, like their male counterparts, concerned with bragging and boasting. "Roxanne's Revenge," the freestyle debut of Roxanne Shanté, answered UTFO's hit "Roxanne, Roxanne," with often-hilarious rhymes but a serious premise: When it came to rhyming, women could match the guys line for line.

The so-called Golden Age of hip-hop in the 1980s was defined by politically conscious groups (Public Enemy, KRS-One, A Tribe Called Quest), and though few women made the scene during this time, the ones who did—including Queen Latifah, MC Lyte, and Monie Love—set a staunchly pro-female agenda. Latifah and Love's 1989 track "Ladies First" demanded admission to the hip-hop boys' club, building on the good-natured razzing of "Roxanne's Revenge" with an emphasis that women in rap were sisters, not rivals, to their male counterparts. Elsewhere, Salt-N-Pepa established themselves as savvy, straight-talking advocates of unapologetic sexuality with the club hit "Push It," one of the first hip-hop singles to be nominated for a Grammy. Sister Souljah made her mark as one of the most militant of Public Enemy's members. And male-female rap collectives such as Digable Planets and Arrested Development added a jazzy, up-with-people facet to the ever-more-dimensional genre.

During the '90s, however, "gangsta rap," with its hypermasculine, ultraviolent lyrical content and cross-cultural appeal, began pushing women to the sidelines in earnest. Women in gangsta rap, unless they were your mama, were "bitches," "tricks," and "hos"; rap videos on MTV and BET began featuring women as literal set decoration. Queen Latifah and Salt-N-Pepa, as well as new voices such as those of Bahamadia and Rah Digga, released albums to critical acclaim, but as the genre grew more commercial, the strongest voices were male ones. According to Tricia Rose, author of 1994's *Black Noise: Rap Music and Black Culture in Contemporary America*, the woman-positive consciousness of Golden Age females such as Latifah and Lyte simply didn't play in a marketplace intent on selling the most outlaw vision of hip-hop to young, male, and often white audiences.

As hip-hop became big business, subject matter that had once been heavily political became almost exclusively commercial. Male and female stars alike rapped about brand-name labels, top-shelf liquor, and gang-ster heroes and heroines. Lil' Kim and Foxy Brown, two of the biggest female rappers of the mid- and late '90s, styled themselves as the hip-hop version of mafia princesses and rhyming strippers. Money was the bottom line, their lyrics suggested, and they would stop at nothing to get it.

Lil' Kim and Foxy weren't the only game in town, of course: Missy Elliott added a sorely needed element of whimsy to rap with her nonsense rhymes and Hefty-bag couture, while Lauryn Hill of the Fugees and Eve, formerly of the rap posse Ruff Ryders, combined sleek R&B singing with her rhymes.

Still, the ever-more-commercial genre made it hard for women whose lyrical concerns ran deeper than a glass of Cristal to hit it big. As Rose put it in a June 2007 edition of NPR's *News & Notes*, "Women MCs are under an enormous amount of pressure to fit a very narrow mold." And though there's a diverse array of celebrated contemporary female rappers, from Ursula Rucker, Aya De Leon, and the Coup's Pam the Funkstress to Jean Grae and J-Ro, it may be some time before these women reach the peaks that their earlier sisters once did. But no one's sleeping on women in hip-hop. Robust dialogues and debates on campuses and in communities take on the complexities of women's production of and representation in hip-hop. And a growing body of work by academics and writers, including Joan Morgan, T. Denean Sharpley-Whiting, Yvonne Bynoe, and Akiba Solomon, prioritizes a feminist analysis of hip-hop, and lobbying groups and nonprofits (such as Industry Ears and the Essence Take Back the Music cam-paign) have made it possible to hear a new Golden Age forming right before our ears.

© Getty Images

Queen Latifah was at the forefront of hip-hop artists whose lyrics set a pro-female agenda.

wave—"the personal is political"—put firmly into practice; as Walker wrote in the introduction to *To Be Real*, "I believe our lives are the best basis for feminist theory."

But just as "third wave" was gaining traction as a descriptor, a competing term was entering the popular lexicon. The word "postfeminism" had been kicked around academic circles since the early 1980s as a feminist theory that was based largely on the idea of gender as a practice rather than an essential facet of one's existence. As early as 1982, mainstream media also began to use the expression to denote women who recognized and appreciated what feminism had brought about, but who didn't see themselves as feminists; the *New York Times* published a story called "Voices from the Post-Feminist Generation," in which young, college-educated, and largely middle-class women opined on the "incredible bitterness" of the feminists who came before them. "Postfeminism," as used in media discourse, served not to talk about the continuing ways that feminism was a necessary and mobilizing force in women's lives but to brush off feminism as a movement that had outlived its usefulness.

To say that postfeminism co-opted third wave feminism isn't quite accurate, but it certainly played a part in hijacking the dialogue that self-identified third wave feminists wanted to have with the culture at large. Leslie Heywood and Jennifer Drake, who edited the 1997 anthology *Third Wave Agenda: Being Feminist, Doing Feminism*, noted in their introduction that third wave feminism had no choice but to contain multitudes in its approach to theory: "Because our lives have been shaped by struggles between various feminisms as well as by cultural backlash against feminism and activism, we argue that contradiction . . . marks the strategies and desires of third wave feminists." This is a very different statement from that delivered by Lily James, cofounder of the website Postfeminist Playground, who expounded on postfeminism in a *PopMatters* interview: "Postfeminism is a lack of interest in chanting the old slogans, waving the old banners, crabbing over the old injustices. Young women today want to exploit and enjoy our freedom, not pout about what freedoms we don't or didn't have. . . . Postfeminists want to move on from feminism—that's the simplest way I can define it. We're tired of being told if we wear makeup and have fun we're betraying our gender and pandering to men. We can go to college, get jobs, do anything we want. The time for crabbing and bitching is over."

The mainstream press had made feminist-bashing into something like a sport for years; newspapers and magazines seemed intent on declaring feminism dead, dying, or irrelevant in articles with lurid titles such as "Requiem for the Women's Movement" (*Harper's*, 1976), "When Feminism Failed" (the *New York Times*, 1988), and "Feminists Have Killed Feminism" (*Los Angeles Times*, 1992). By 1998, it seemed impossible to ignore that feminism was thriving on college campuses, in blue-chip nonprofits such as NOW and the Feminist Majority, in activist communities both large (Third Wave Foundation) and small (Radical Cheerleaders), and in a number of publications in print (*Bust*, *Bitch*, *Hues Maxine*) and on the Internet (gURL, Wench). And yet, the mandate of what Jennifer Pozner has called "False Feminist Death Syndrome" was to ignore all this, to champion "postfeminism," and, in the case of *Time* magazine, to publish perhaps the most egregious article to date on how feminism had supposedly failed.

The cover that illustrated the 1998 story "It's All About Me!" featured four feminist icons: Susan B. Anthony, Betty Friedan, Gloria Steinem, and . . . Ally McBeal. Its author, Ginia Bellafante, alleged that the gains of the women's movement in the 1960s and '70s were in danger of being undone by a new strain of feminism that was typified by the "narcissistic rambling of a few, media-anointed spokeswomen." Bellafante complained that "if feminism of the '60s and '70s was steeped in research and obsessed with social change, feminism today is wed to the culture of celebrity and self-obsession."

This claim may have held more water if Bellafante had been more rigorous in her own research—say, seeking out any number of grassroots activists who would have been happy to talk to her about how their work was a continuation of the projects begun by the women of the second wave. But instead, Bellafante quoted the very celebrities she derided (such as Courtney Love) as well as a few whose careers were built precisely on pooh-poohing the social-change feminism she referred to so piously (such as Camille Paglia and Katie Roiphe, neither of whom align themselves with the feminist movement, instead advocating for individual social responsibility). Furthermore, the premise of Bellafante's article was flawed in her choice of icon; like many reporters who would come after her, she held up the fictional Ally McBeal as evidence that feminism was dead. Any number of heads could have rested beside Steinem's on that *Time* cover: Rebecca Walker of the Third Wave Foundation; Riot Grrrl figurehead Kathleen Hanna; feminist folkie Ani DiFranco. But Ally's tiny noggin was a much more convenient symbol to denote the failure of feminism. (Right around the time this cover story appeared, columnist Barbara Ehrenreich—as steeped-in-research-and-obsessed-with-social-change a feminist as Bellafante could have hoped to find—was relieved of her job at *Time*.)

Naturally, actual feminists weren't having this; *Time* received so many letters in response to the article that the magazine devoted a special section to them. This, in itself, was evidence that the article had struck a deeply discordant note. One response, in the online journal *Salon*, summed up the problem with Bellafante's article: Feminists had broadened the very substance of feminist dialogue, and it was up to onlookers such as Bellafante to keep up rather than dismiss out of hand anything that didn't look like "traditional" feminism—which itself was too often reduced to the marching of white, middle-class women. As author Janelle Brown wrote in her *Salon* article "Is *Time* Brain-Dead?": "[T]he new generations of feminists have found their own issues: sexuality, media representations of women, what it means to be female in a world that feels that women must be either lipstick fashion babes or bitchy feminists, with no room for anything in between. And though Bellafante breezily ignores them, there are plenty of women who are writing about glass ceilings and international politics—it's just not the only issue they're focusing on anymore."

Responses such as these pointed out the central and most frustrating theme in the cultural coverage of feminism and feminists: The issues covered were the sexiest, most controversial, or most damning ones. Sexuality and sex work, rape, and beauty standards got the nod; still-unresolved classics such as the wage gap and other forms of institutionalized sexism were glossed over or ignored. The interactions between feminism and pop culture had become a long hall of warped mirrors, each one reflecting the distortions of the ones before. Feminism at the turn of the century was perhaps richer and more varied than it had ever been before—but feminists were finding themselves continually battling a media that didn't want that news getting around. If it were possible for feminism and pop culture to be both entwined and at loggerheads, that was the state of things as both phenomena moved into the new century.

CHAPTER 5

WOMEN UNDER THE INFLUENCE: POP CULTURE NOW AND BEYOND

BY THE DAWN OF THE NEW CENTURY, women were living in what could be called a deceptively postfeminist moment. That is to say, feminism was widely considered to be "done": We had a handful of female CEOs in major corporations, a sturdy bloc of senators, governors, and congresswomen—even two women on the Supreme Court. Women weren't held back from college or graduate school; they were, in fact, encouraged. "What's the problem?" people wanted to know. Hadn't we gotten everything we asked for? Why were we still whining about sexism? Didn't we know how good we had it? For god's sake, *what did women want?*

Well, for starters, what many women wanted was a swift end to the mistaken notion that all of feminism's goals had magically been achieved. And for these women, it was time for a comprehensive, old-school approach—a mission statement for what women's activism would look like in the year 2000 and beyond. Two books were crucial in laying out talking points for this future feminism and in emphasizing that the terms of feminist dialogue had changed indelibly. The books, 2000's *Manifesta: Young Women, Feminism, and the Future*, and 2002's *Colonize This! Young Women of Color on Today's Feminism*, extensively discussed the ways that individual experience colored feminist and antiracist theory, the need to bridge what seemed to be a growing generational rift in feminism, and the undeniable reality that different understandings of feminism shouldn't hold women back from identifying as a feminist. These weren't new ideas, of course—many of them had been kicked around since the 1970s. The key now was to make sure these understandings of feminism weren't left on the fringes—to move them, as bell hooks put it, "from margin to center."

Putting feminist issues front and center wasn't the easiest task, unfortunately, in large part because of resistance from the media and popular culture. In many ways, the public perception and processing of feminism had changed little since the Women's Strike for Equality: If a feminist issue or event were up for discussion in the media, you could bet that the most prominent voices involved wouldn't be those of actual feminists. Sure, mainstream organs such as *Newsweek* and *Time* made perfunctory efforts to ring up the offices of NOW and *Ms.* for quotes on, say, women in the military or the possibility of a *Roe v. Wade* rollback, but increasingly, media makers seemed to be under the impression that since they didn't see a young Gloria Steinem on their narrow radar, feminism had no new spokeswomen. Increasingly, the most visible and most quoted experts on feminism, in fact, weren't feminist activists such as Amy Richards and Jennifer Baumgardner (*Manifesta*'s authors), or Daisy Hernández and Bushra Rehman (the editors of *Colonize This!*), but women who didn't actually identify as feminists at all—and who in fact were quick to blame feminism for all society's ills. And, as ever, the mainstream media was a lot more inspired to cover the subject of woman-on-woman antipathy as aired in books such as Christina Hoff Sommers's *The War Against Boys: How Misguided Feminism Is Harming Our Young Men* (thesis: Feminism has gone too far with feminizing everything) or Danielle Crittenden's *What Our Mothers Didn't Tell Us* (feminism makes women unhappy because it tells them to postpone marriage and childrearing) than it was to give voice to a thriving, youth-driven feminist resurgence.

The central problem in getting the word out about feminism was that an effective feminism needed to critique commercialism and consumerism; it needed to pull no punches in calling out the beauty industry, women's magazines, Wall Street, Hollywood, and Madison Avenue as perpetual realms of oppression. But it also needed a commercial, consumer approach to appeal to all the people it hoped to reach—it needed to get reviewed in newspapers that people read, TV that everyone watched, books that Oprah talked about. To succeed, feminism needed to do the equivalent of going into Starbucks, buying a triple venti latte, and then passing out flyers about why other customers should boycott Starbucks. The eternal question—can you dismantle the master's house with the master's tools?—was more puzzling than ever now that the master's house seemed riddled with booby traps.

The World According to Reality TV

Feminism still had plenty of battles to fight in the realm of pop cultural representation, and the new millennium had introduced a doozy of a new antagonist: so-called "reality television." The first of the new guard of reality shows immediately struck fear into the hearts of feminists everywhere, at least the ones who had pop culture on their radar. It was called *Who Wants to Marry a Multi-Millionaire?* and it sprang from the mean-spirited notion that women were so shallow and so mercenary that they would line up to marry a man about whom they knew absolutely nothing except his alleged net worth. On the two-hour extravaganza, fifty women were paraded, beauty pageant–style, around a Las Vegas stage, while their would-be husband surveyed them, unseen, from afar. Once he'd made his pick, he was revealed, and the couple were legally married on the spot. The premise was meant to be outrageous, the viewers repeatedly encouraged to wonder, *Who were these women? What would make them think this was a good idea? Had they no self-respect? Why can't I stop watching this train wreck?*

In an unsurprising aftermath, the show was revealed to have skimped on the honesty: The titular multimillionaire, it turned out, was a struggling actor who was not only not rich, but who had a disturbing history with women. (A quick background check turned up at least one ex-girlfriend with a restraining order against him.) And yet, the premise of *Who Wants to Marry a Multi-Millionaire?*—namely, that it's super fun to watch women compete with each other for the affections of a man they barely know—was quickly rejiggered and shopped to other networks by Mike Fleiss, one of its producers. In 2002, a softened version

Know Your Antifeminists

The Independent Women's Forum (IWF) is a large, well-funded organiza-tion based in Washington, DC. Its website proclaims that its members are "women who are committed to promoting and defending economic op-portunity and political freedom" and asserts that "for too long, false ideas and ideals about women in America have dominated public discourse. We provide a new voice for American women on where they stand and what they want—for themselves, their families, their communities, and their country."

Sounds pretty good, right? Well, not so fast. The IWF quite consciously uses vague, feminist-friendly language—right down to its name—to mask an avowedly antifeminist agenda. Among other things, the IWF denies the existence of a systemic wage gap, even when acknowledging that women who make 77 cents to the man's dollar have it great (as the group's cur-rent president Carrie Lukas did in a 2007 *Washington Post* column). The IWF is notoriously quiet on the subject of abortion, though it opposes com-prehensive sex education in schools and vocally tsk-tsks the concept of women's sexual agency. And it's been outspoken in opposing the Violence Against Women Act, which among other things establishes federal fund-ing for domestic-abuse and sexual-assault resources for women, men, and children. One of the IWF's most vocal members, Christina Hoff Som-mers, has written not one but two feminist-blaming books (1994's *Who Stole Feminism? How Women Have Betrayed Women* and 2000's *The War Against Boys: How Misguided Feminism Is Harming Our Young Men*).

Deliberately putting forth a savvy, independent facade is in fact the hall-mark of more than a few antifeminists. There's writer Camille Paglia, who considers herself a lone voice of reason in a sea of political correctness and moral prudery. Paglia's books, however—among them 1990's *Sexual*

of the show made its debut, this time featuring a handsome, rich single guy who week by week would whittle down his harem until the last one standing got an engagement ring. Though *Who Wants to Marry a Multi-Millionaire?* had been derided for its rank chauvinism and crassness, *The Bachelor*, despite its nearly identical premise, was received much more kindly, and pretty soon every network was scrambling to create its

Personae, 1992's *Sex, Art, and American Culture*, and 2005's *Break, Blow, Burn*—blame feminism for the stunted landscape of American art and culture, insisting that feminism has sought to change men's essential nature and in so doing drained the creativity and power that's a natural result of men's animal sexuality. Her contention that women should be responsible for not getting raped, meanwhile, is at odds with her firmly held belief that men are predisposed to do it: Among her other bits of rape apologia is this gem: "Feminism . . . does not see what is for men the eroticism or fun element in rape, especially the wild, infectious delirium of gang rape." Then there are folks such as writer Caitlin Flanagan and right-wing *National Review* editor Kate O'Beirne, self-styled pundits who have built careers writing about how feminists have devalued the roles of wife and mother, and that the best job a woman can do is raise and take care of a family. Yet—fancy that!—both women are or have been working mothers themselves. How convenient for them.

No one is arguing that these women shouldn't exist or voice their opinions. What's problematic is that their points of view are the ones so frequently aired in mainstream debates about feminism—or worse, are simply considered "the women's perspective" on such topics as family and working motherhood. Why has Flanagan been given oodles of space in well-respected, ostensibly left-leaning publications such as the *Atlantic Monthly* and the *New Yorker* to write antifeminist polemics? Why did the *Atlantic* excerpt *The War Against Boys*, but not, say, Susan Faludi's *Stiffed*, a book released the same year that also dealt with feminism's effect on men? Where the words of both feminists and antifeminists are published makes a huge difference in how they influence our culture: If antifeminists such as Rush Limbaugh or Ann Coulter, for instance, were simply people standing on a street corner wearing sandwich boards and shouting "Liberals die!" into megaphones made of a paper-towel rolls, today's pop culture might look a lot different.

own version. They came in rapid and increasingly contrived succession: *Temptation Island, Mr. Personality, For Love or Money, Joe Millionaire, Married by America, Love Cruise, Paradise Hotel*. The formula wasn't always the same—*Mr. Personality* and *Average Joe*, for instance, flipped the gender setup, presenting a single woman who was wooed by men in creepy colored masks (the show was about personality, not looks, you see) and men who were kind of dorky, respectively; *Temptation Island* marooned feuding young couples on an island and provided them with tons of booze and single hotties to cheat with; *Joe Millionaire* duped its female participants into believing its construction-worker hero was really a millionaire in hopes that it would up the drama. As voice-overs gleefully announced, "The claws will come out!" and wondered, "Who will be sent home brokenhearted?" viewers were treated to a spectacle of desperate women falling all over themselves to please a man because literally winning his affection—even for a few minutes in a hot tub—was the most important thing in the world. The women themselves were sadly uniform—almost always white, in their early twenties, and devoid of anything resembling a personality, though it's only fair to mention that the men they fought over weren't blessed in that department either. The few women of color who popped up in each show rarely made it very far before being cut loose, perhaps because engaging with the subject of interracial dating would require the show to present real conversations between the participants, something that never seemed to happen.

Jennifer Pozner, who founded the nonprofit media-monitoring organization Women in Media and News, argued in a 2004 *Ms.* article, "The Unreal World," that though these shows were promoted—chiefly to women—as "guilty pleasures," there was a sinister undercurrent of backlash written into their narratives. She wrote that reality TV shows convey the message that "no emotional, professional or political accomplishment can possibly compare with the twin vocations of beauty and marriage.

"Apologists claim reality TV isn't sexist because no one forces women to appear on these shows. But the impact on the shows' participants is almost beside the point: The real concern is the millions of viewers, scores of whom are young girls, who take in these misogynistic spectacles uncritically, learning that only the most stereotypically beautiful, least independent women with the lowest-carb diets will be rewarded with love, financial security and the ultimate prize of male validation."

Were these shows ushering in new stores of antifeminist sentiment?

Did their existence cancel out the feminist work being done by grassroots organizations and political action groups? In most cases, a gendered power imbalance was the very basis of these reality TV shows. And as Pozner pointed out, the simple repetition of tropes and assumptions put forth by these shows couldn't help but have an impact on their viewers—and their viewers were most likely young women. Pozner, who has traveled the country since 2002 speaking on college campuses about reality TV, noted in a 2007 PBS interview that when she first began doing campus talks, reality dating shows were new and jarring to viewers—a source of frustration and consistent debate about women, gender roles, racism, and media responsibility. However, as such shows became more copious and less novel, students became less outraged. Reality TV, sexist or not, was simply another item in a buffet of pop culture that they were encouraged to consume voraciously.

It's not that feminists expected I-am-woman-hear-me-roar sentiments from shows in which the bikinis had more personality than their wearers. It's more that women expected TV portrayals of themselves to move forward, not backward—with more diversity, more independence, more smarts, more nuance. There are, of course, a consistent crop of women represented on television in ways that are in line with reality—the district attorneys and medical examiners on *Law and Order*, the forensic experts of *CSI* and *Bones*, the undercover cops of *The Wire*, and the doctors of *ER* and *House*. Even women in traditional roles of wives and mothers were, on shows such as *The Sopranos*, *Six Feet Under*, and *Soul Food*, much more finely drawn and complex than ever before. But reality TV was such an unstoppable moneymaker—shows were cheap, easy to produce, and attractive to advertisers, whose products were often showcased on the programs themselves—that they soon outnumbered traditional narrative television shows on almost every network. And soon enough, it seemed that for every smart, stable, and competent woman on television, there were a dozen squealing, weeping women who wanted nothing more than to marry a man they'd never met, bed a rock star, or become a Playboy Bunny or Pussycat Doll.

If only feminists could ignore these shows. Many did, of course, but it was at their peril. Because reality competitions varying from *The Bachelor* to *American Idol* had revolutionized TV (in the case of the former, single-handedly saving the ABC network from financial free fall), their import was constantly mulled over in the media in discussions of things like narcissism, racism, and class anxiety. A 2003 article in *Newsweek* titled "Spinsterhood Is Powerful" considered the gender flip wrought by *The Bachelor*'s sister show, *The Bachelorette*; its author, Marc Peyser, seemed doubtful that twenty-five bachelors could sink to the depths of self-loathing humiliation that female competitors did, wondering, "What's the point of 'The Bachelorette' if no one gets reduced to a bitter, blubbering fool on national television?" Elsewhere in the article, Peyser notes that producer Mike Fleiss created the show to answer the many critiques of *The Bachelor*'s inherent sexism, which revealed just how faulty Hollywood's notion of feminism actually was.

Choosing Your Choice: Mandatory Empowerment and Pop Culture

The ascent of reality TV has brought us a rash of shows that traffic in broadly drawn concepts of "empowerment" and "actualization." These tend to be the ones that focus on makeovers, whether sartorial or more far-reaching: *Extreme Makeover* (in which people got extensive overhauls via graphically portrayed cosmetic surgeries), *What Not to Wear* (in which fashion "don'ts" are taught how to shop and their wardrobes rehabbed by two sassy stylists), *How Do I Look?* (wherein friends and family of a struggling style case shop for makeover looks for her—it's almost always a her).

The show that took the proverbial cake in this genre was the two-season mind-boggler known as *The Swan*. A kind of Frankenshow that combined elements of *Extreme Makeover*, *Oprah*, and the Miss America Pageant, *The Swan* went something like this: First, find a group of twenty- and thirtysomething women who are unhappy with their fat thighs, crooked teeth, acne scars, postpregnancy bellies, and flat bottoms. Second, make sure they all have personal issues—maybe an inability to enjoy sex, strained relationships with their parents, or a verbally or even physically abusive boyfriend. Third, herd the women into tiny apartments with all reflective surfaces removed or covered. Fourth, have them evaluated by a team that includes glib cosmetic and dental surgeons, a personal trainer, a psychologist, and a bully (a.k.a. the show's producer), who will allegedly work with them during the course of the show to "transform them from the inside out." Fifth, get to work making them over with extensive procedures—liposuction and tummy tucks; breast, chin, butt, and cheekbone implants; rhinoplasties and eyelid lifts; teeth caps and gum surgery; and collagen injections and laser hair removal—and put them each on a diet.

Each week, viewers were treated to the spectacle of bandaged Swans hobbling around their tiny rooms with faces so swollen and bruised they couldn't eat (all the better to shed that pesky weight!), whimpering through phone calls with children who wanted to know when they were coming home, and enduring sessions with the shows' psychologist and life coach, whose version of changing the contestants from the inside out seemed to begin and end with hectoring them about "sticking with the program." Once the women had healed up, it was time for each one to be revealed simultaneously to herself and to the audience at home. Before showing each woman the first mirror she's seen in weeks, the show's host recapped how terrible she'd looked and felt before her *Swan*-ification. And then, finally, we saw the mirror and the inevitable tears and disbelief as each contestant looked at her new face and body, running her hands all over herself as if she were a trophy. And once each woman's insecurities had ostensibly been banished through the wonders of science, the *Swan* team couldn't wait to bring those insecurities back with a flourish. Two women were made over each episode; after the reveal, one was deemed to have "made more progress" than the other, and that lucky gal got to stick around for the big finish: a beauty pageant.

Amazingly, the show's producers had the chutzpah to call this parade of what amounted to competitive plastic surgery both liberating and therapeutic for women. Woman after woman spoke of the plans she had for her new self, in work and love and beyond—as though it simply wouldn't have been okay for her less conventionally attractive former self to have such plans. On each episode, the beauty ideal that was reinforced was one that was literally constructed, and the women told that the very fakeness they bought into was what would liberate them.

More recently, other reality shows have broadened the definition of just what competitive activities are considered liberating and empowering for women. Exhibit A: *Pussycat Dolls Present: The Search for the Next Doll*, wherein a gaggle of women compete for the honor of joining a burlesque troupe cum singing group whose biggest hits have asked the listener, "Dontcha wish your girlfriend was hot like me?" and urged him to "loosen up my buttons." The group is a sort of Spice Girls 2.0, only instead of "girl power," its members shill something more akin to "hot power." On its surface, *The Search for the Next Doll* isn't unlike *America's Next Top Model*, which is also based on the pursuit of hotness. The difference is that no *Top Model* hopeful has ever stated that standing around in a bikini is "all about female empowerment," as one of the would-be Dolls did in the premiere episode of the show; its executive producer, a man who goes only by "McG," went on to extol the competition as "a snapshot of the contemporary woman being everything she can be."

McG, knowingly or not, had hit on one of the chief forms of conflict and debate within third wave feminism: the question of choice. As an ideology, feminism has from the start been about choice—about making sure women had choices (to vote, to work, to be an autonomous person and not the property of a father or husband) and about showing how those choices contributed to a society in which personal and civil rights were protected. In the years since the landmark case *Roe v. Wade* went to the Supreme Court, and abortion was referred to as "this choice" in the court's majority ruling, the word had become most closely aligned with the protection of reproductive rights, specifically women's right to a safe and legal abortion. But as Rickie Solinger pointed out in her book *Beggars and Choosers: How the Politics of Choice Shapes Adoption, Abortion, and Welfare in the United States*, "choice" was a deliberately

Producers and contestants alike on The Pussycat Dolls Present: The Search for the Next Doll *argued that the performance group is all about female empowerment.*

apolitical use of language, substituted for the more militant-sounding "rights" to lessen the perceived impact of the court's decision: "In a country weary of rights claims, choice became *the* way liberal and mainstream feminists could talk about abortion without mentioning the 'A-word.' Many people believed that 'choice'—a term that evoked women shoppers selecting among options in the marketplace—would be an easier sell; it offered 'rights lite,' a package less threatening or disturbing than unadulterated rights."

In the early years of the 2000s, abortion was once again in question thanks to a deeply conservative presidential administration that didn't conceal its hope of repealing *Roe*, but now the word "choice" was being used in a slightly different way. As Summer Wood pointed out in a 2004 article in *Bitch*, "The word's primacy in the reproductive-rights arena has slowly caused the phrase 'It's my choice' to become synonymous with 'It's a feminist thing to do'—or, perhaps more precisely, 'It is antifeminist to criticize my decision.' The result has been a rapid depoliticizing of 'choice' and an often misguided application of feminist ideology to consumer imperatives, invoked not only for the right to decide whether to undergo abortion, but also for the right to undergo cosmetic surgery, for example, or to buy all manner of products marketed to women, from cigarettes to antidepressants to diet frozen pizzas." Was "choice" now shorthand for "feminism"? Was any choice at all a feminist choice if the person who made it invoked feminism? Furthermore, was it antifeminist to question whether "choices" that bought into industries routinely critiqued by feminists for their limited conceptions of womanhood—such as the choice to get a boob job or to put on little more than hot pants and gyrate for the chance to become a Pussycat Doll—really typified what feminism should be? And in a world where women were in real danger of losing the original choice granted by *Roe*, could less-substantial choices remain a viable stand-in for feminist ideology? The state of "choice" soon became a source of both confusion and mirth, culminating in a headline in the satirical publication *The Onion* that read "Women Now Empowered by Everything a Woman Does." ("Today's woman lives in a near-constant state of empowerment," enthused the accompanying article.)

Reality television wasn't the only pop culture phenomenon that invoked choice to reify expectations of women that were far from revolutionary. Slowly but surely, the culture itself was proposing a new way women could empower themselves—or was it just a new twist on an age-old expectation?

Do-Me Feminism and the Rise of Raunch

Constructing a politics of pleasure has been key to third wave feminism. Thanks to their brave and often unsettling analyses of sexual power structures and the connections between pornography and a larger system of male dominance, feminists of the 1960s and '70s had gotten roundly tarred as being antisex, antiporn, antiheterosexual, and just generally prudish. In part to address this stereotype, the interest in feminist theories of sexuality and the development of a prosex politics became one of the strongest threads of feminism throughout the 1990s and the

2000s. Feminists have debated age-old virgin-whore dichotomies, have called for representations of alternative sexualities and of heterosexuality as experienced by people of all colors and abilities, and have offered controversial-but-compelling perspectives on the power dynamics of everything from butch/femme to S/M. That said, promoting pleasure for women has been as frustrating as it is crucial, thanks in large part to a media and pop culture that still depends on—and overwhelmingly presents—a limited view of female sexuality riddled with moralism, judgment, and classic double standards.

Take the phrase "Do-me feminism," coined by journalist Tad Friend in a 1994 *Esquire* article called "Feminist Women Who Like Sex," which name-checked the likes of Susie Bright, Naomi Wolf, bell hooks, Pat (now Patrick) Califia, and Lisa Palac, writers whose work was concerned with, among other things, creating a broader, more inclusive sexual paradigm. Some of these authors had written previously about feeling that their interest in sex, especially heterosexual sex, made them outsiders in a feminist world that ostensibly believed "Not all rape is intercourse, but all intercourse is rape" (a sentiment falsely but repeatedly attributed to famed antipornography activists Andrea Dworkin and Catharine MacKinnon). Wolf famously wrote in her book *Fire with Fire: The New Female Power and How It Will Change the 21st Century* that she finds shelter and solace in the male body, and that "there is an elaborate vocabulary in which to describe sexual harm done by men, but almost no vocabulary in which a woman can celebrate sex with men."

Friend's piece picked up on these quotes to construct a straw-woman argument against the dogmatic, antisex profile of second wave feminists and to subsequently champion the women who were supposedly "beating their swords into bustiers" and expressing their feminism one amazing blow job at time. The article's title said it all—in identifying "feminist women who like sex," *Esquire* implied that, as a rule, feminist women don't like sex. And ultimately, the piece was service journalism, not so much intended to open an informed dialogue about sex as to convey via heavy breathing that, Hey guys! Hot feminist

What the L?

Before *The L Word*, lesbians functioned as a kind of edgy set dressing in television, deployed for yuks and male discomfort on sitcoms (see Ross's ex-wife on *Friends*) or for a dramatic, often male-identified sexual thrill on prime-time dramas (see *L.A. Law* or *Fastlane*) and reality shows. So when Showtime premiered its hour-long ensemble drama in 2004, it was a TV landmark.

Still, being the first for-lesbians, by-lesbians TV show (among its writers and producers were Rose Troche and Guinevere Turner, the director and star, respectively, of classic lesbian indie film *Go Fish*) meant that a whole lot of people were expecting *The L Word* to be all things to all lesbians. And as you might expect, there's been very little consensus since the show came on the air about whether its glossy, stylish take on L.A. power lesbians—with a few questioning heteros, staunch bisexuals, and FTM trans-sexuals in the mix as well—actually reflects the larger LGBT community.

Plenty of people, for instance, scorned the fact that nearly every player in this Sapphic soap looked as though she'd stepped out of the pages of *Glamour* and faulted the show for superimposing conventional hetero beauty standards on otherwise daring plot points about bi- and transphobia, bondage and domination, and race. But others applauded this very thing, arguing that it was helpful to offer unwitting watchers a view of lesbians that didn't conflate sexual preference with gender confusion—and that didn't involve shapeless pants, acid-washed denim vests, and mullets.

Some viewers were impatient to see butch representation to balance the show's phalanx of femmes, still more grew impatient with its apparent lack of class consciousness, and plenty just couldn't take all the melodrama: The breakups! The cheating! The baby stealing! The out-of-nowhere cancer! (Almost everyone could, however, agree on one thing: The theme song was *terrible*.) After each episode, online discussion boards, such as those on snarky fan favorite Television Without Pity, teemed with back-and-forth about the plot points, the characterizations, and the copious sex scenes.

As the first TV show to show lesbians simply living—affirming what Adrienne Rich called "lesbian existence" in a mainstream entertainment forum—*The L Word*, flawed or not, serves a crucial purpose. With any luck, it will be joined by a whole spectrum of shows that do so in bigger, better ways than it ever imagined.

women want to have sex with you! And thus, a new feminism entered the mainstream—leading with its breasts—and became a key example of why feminism just couldn't be easily translated into mainstream media formulas.

This idea of do-me feminism as the dominant identity of the third wave extended to a rekindled interest in the intersections of feminism and sex work. The idea that sex-based economies could grapple with and engage in feminism was not a new one; it had been limned in the mid-1990s by the likes of *On Our Backs* magazine and in the thoughtful work of authors such as Bright, Califia, Palac, Carol Queen, and Annie Sprinkle. The 1997 anthology *Whores and Other Feminists* offered a bracing look at how the worlds of peep shows, stripping, prostitution, domination/submission, and porn professionals interact with feminism in both theory and practice. The book's editor, Jill Nagle, was inspired to collect such stories by a roundtable on the sex industry in a 1994 issue of *Ms.* magazine that featured only one participant who had actually been involved in sex work—the notoriously rigid, if impressively impassioned, Dworkin. In an interview with the online literary magazine *Beatrice*, Nagle clarified why she so badly wanted the book out in the world:

> *A lot of feminists come to the [antiporn] position through having experienced what it's like to be treated as a sexual object inappropriately. . . . It's a natural—and I think a necessary—response. . . . [But] sex isn't just a world of danger, it's a world of possibilities as well. The point of saying no to danger is to be able to say yes to pleasure. The kind of feminism engendered in what the sex workers I know are doing is going to change the face of feminism if word ever gets out, so I've put it upon myself to get the word out.*

Unfortunately, as with so much of feminism, the word that got out about feminism and sex work was devoid of the kind of nuance found in *Whores* or the feminist writing that came before it. Instead of engaging with theories of how sex work subverts heteronormativity or offering dialogues about the intersections of race, class, and capitalism, what the media and pop culture filtered from these works was the simplistic equation that it was now a feminist act to strip for a living or to watch porn.

Magazines and newspapers all over the world scrambled to spread the news. Two self-proclaimed feminists in New York City founded the group CAKE, whose sole mission was to throw parties at which women wore as little as they wanted, danced on bars with each other, and allowed men to watch as long as they were accompanied by a CAKE member. Websites such as SuicideGirls and Burning Angel popped up on the Internet, offering pinups and porn that didn't conform to pneumatic San Fernando Valley stereotypes; instead of beachy-looking blonds with airbrushed studio tans and cosmetically engorged breasts, these websites showcased different flavors of "alternative" pinups, from sullen, skinny goth girls to tattooed, pierced gutter punks. The cable channel HBO suddenly seemed to have a show about stripping, prostitution, or the porn industry on offer every night of the week. Even *Playboy* was no longer looked upon as sexist—after all, it was run by a woman, so how could it be? The idea went like so: By "performing" sex work—that is, knowingly enacting what was expected of a stripper or other sex worker—women were in fact reclaiming a sexuality that had been the property of men and using it for themselves. It was objectification as anticipatory retaliation: They were taking back that male gaze and making money off it to boot.

The bedrock arguments for sex work as feminist came down to the concepts of "choice"—of course—and financial independence. Supporters of sex work as a feminist act noted that women in the porn industry typically get paid far more than men, and that strippers earned much more in one evening than they could in a week working a manual-labor or retail job. Those who argued for it as a choice reasoned that sex work wasn't all that different from waitressing anyway.

Of course, not everyone was down with pop culture's heavy-breathing embrace of this new take on feminism. For one thing, some feminists were quick to note that HBO's salacious exposés such as *G-String Divas*, or *Salon*'s publication of high-class call girl Tracy Quan's weekly column, portrayed only the women who actually *did* have a choice. Women who were driven by systemic poverty or abuse—who were sex workers for survival—were invariably absent from any girl-powery narratives of how stripping helped women embrace their sexuality/imperfect bodies/previously shameful kinky streak. For another, very little ink was given to the larger structure of commercial sex work. For instance, SuicideGirls cofounder Missy Suicide insisted that her site was "absolutely feminist," citing as proof that half the site's subscribers are female, and that the models on the site control their own photo shoots and imagery. But she didn't note that models were paid a paltry $200 for photo sets that the site's founders—unbeknownst to the models—then turned around and sold to other sites, pocketing the profits. (The site's practices came to light in 2005, when models began leaving the site en masse.) And as sex worker Sarah Katherine Lewis noted in a 2007 *AlterNet* article, the equation of sex work + money = feminism was a little too simple.

> *The unglamorous truth about my experience as an adult entertainer is that I felt empowered—as a woman, as a feminist, and as a human being—by the money I made, not by the work I did. The performances I gave didn't change anyone's ideas about women. On the contrary, I was in the business of reinforcing the same old sexist misinformation. . . . I wasn't "owning" or "subverting" anything other than my own working-class status. Bending over to Warrant's "Cherry Pie" didn't make me a better feminist. It just made me a feminist who could afford her own rent.*

Lewis noted that, as a working-class woman, she was "lucky" to have the choice of stripping for a living. But her statement posed the question of why self-objectification—never mind how fun or empowering it might be—was the most financially remunerative option for women who wanted to make a good living despite limited resources, education, and time.

Ariel Levy's 2005 book *Female Chauvinist Pigs: Women and the Rise of Raunch Culture* argued that, in fact, women themselves were turning to self-objectification in shocking numbers, noting that the signifiers of what she called "raunch culture"—strip aerobics classes, T-shirts printed with the words PORN STAR, *Girls Gone Wild*, and more—had been adopted by women themselves. But rather than leading to real freedom, women's adoption of "raunch culture" simply duplicated patterns of disdain for and objectification of women. Levy's quest to find out how the new sexual liberation differed from early-model sexploitation involved talking to everyone from the HBO executives responsible for the likes of *G-String Divas* to the producers of *Girls Gone Wild* to high-school and college women who have felt pressure to make out with other girls in bars "because boys like it." Ultimately, *Female Chauvinist Pigs* yielded far more questions than it answered, and the main one was this: If the standards and stereotypes by which girls and women are judged haven't changed, could it really be called empowerment at all?

Pamela Paul struggled with a similar question in her 2005 book *Pornified: How Pornography Is Transforming Our Lives, Our Relationships, and Our Families*; a year later, T. Denean Sharpley-Whiting took it on in *Pimps Up, Ho's Down: Hip Hop's Hold on Young Black Women*. Along with *Female Chauvinist Pigs*, these books pointed out the distinction that lay at the heart of many feminists' discomfort with raunch culture: Liking sex and performing sex are two very different things. And as Levy put it, "If we're going to have sexual role models, it should be the women who enjoy sex the most, not the women who get paid the most to enact it."

Sex work and empowerment will likely remain one of the defining debates of contemporary feminism—much like past (and to many minds still unresolved) questions about the place of heterosexual marriage or labor politics in feminism. But in a larger realm of pop culture, it is worrisome to see that the visual aspects of raunch culture are indeed infectious, reflected in the number of girls and women who submit applications to SuicideGirls, try out to be Pussycat Dolls, and buy into the notion that, for all women's alleged independence and freedom, the most valuable things they can be still hinge on sex appeal.

Real Women and Beyond: Advertising's New Feminism

As I write this, there's a brand-new film short making the rounds of TV and the web. The film is called *Onslaught*, and its first few moments show a dreamy close-up of a young girl—pretty, creamy complexioned, innocent. "Here it comes . . . here it comes . . ." warns the deceptively cheery background music. Then the backbeat kicks in, and the camera zooms toward a montage of images that come so thick and fast they nearly paralyze the eye. Women in bikinis on billboards. Women's body parts—lips, breasts, eyes—in ads on bus shelters and in magazines. A woman on a scale, her body swiftly shrinking and expanding as she gazes down at the magic numbers. Women on surgical gurneys, their problem areas circled with markers and targeted by lasers, scalpels, and liposuction cannulae that are thrust violently in and out of their bodies. Women on TV who promise the product in their hands will make you smaller, thinner, longer, smoother, and leaner. The riot of images is mesmerizing. As it draws to a close and we see more young girls peering into the camera, these words appear on the screen: "Talk to your daughter before the beauty industry does."

Films such as this aren't new; in fact, media activists such as Jean Kilbourne and Sut Jhally have based their careers on them. Kilbourne's documentaries *Killing Us Softly*, *Still Killing Us Softly*, and *Slim Hopes* and Jhally's video series *Dreamworlds* use a barrage of ads to offer a disturbing chronicle of how advertising manipulates women's visions of themselves, teaching them a vigilant hatred of their own bodies that often lasts a lifetime. The difference between Kilbourne and Jhally's work and the video called *Onslaught*, however, is that *Onslaught* is an ad for Dove cosmetics.

More specifically, it's a film produced to draw attention to something called the Dove Self-Esteem Fund, which itself is part of Dove's Campaign for Real Beauty, a global undertaking mounted in 2005 combining marketing, fundraising, and movement politics in an effort to promote a healthier, more inclusive, and just plain celebratory view of women's bodies. The campaign has resulted in ads for Dove products that show women rarely seen in ads for beauty products: women of color, women older than fifty, women with plump or even average-size bodies, women with profuse freckles, women with gray hair or Botox-shunning wrinkles. These ads have asked questions such as "Oversized? Or outstanding?" and "Does true beauty only squeeze into a size 6?" The Dove Self-Esteem Fund was established to encourage the Campaign for Real Beauty from the ground up, underwriting programs designed to raise self-esteem in young women and girls through education.

New Dove Firming. As tested on real curves.

© Redux Pictures

Dove's Campaign for Real Beauty presented images of women who fall outside the realm of conventional standards for advertising models. The ads provoked both appreciation and criticism.

Considering that most ads targeting a female audience unabashedly use a combination of shame and sex appeal for their pitches, the spectacle of a happy-looking, multicultural range of real-life women posing in their undies—the best known of the Campaign for Real Beauty's ads—was undoubtedly a step forward. Or was it? The underwear ads drew fire from various groups of folks in the slew of media coverage that accompanied the campaign in 2005. Newspaper and magazine articles with titles such as "Fab or Flab?" and "When Tush Comes to Dove" worried that the ads would alienate women from a brand that associated itself with "fat girls," and more than a few commentators, citing health-conscious concerns, fretted that a campaign featuring "overweight" women (that is, women of average size) would encourage a growing obesity problem in the United States. On the other hand, women who supported the idea of including meatier women in beauty ads chafed at the fact that Dove's chipper ladies were marketing firming creams and lotions. Others noted that it was difficult to get behind the ads knowing that Dove's parent company (the global brand Unilever) also owned Axe body spray, a product known for its relentlessly sexist ads.

It's in this context that the Dove Self-Esteem Fund has released viral ads such as *Onslaught* and an earlier spot called *Evolution*, which used the filmmaking trick of time-lapsing to show a model being transformed, first through makeup and then through Photoshop, for a billboard spot. The goal of such spots is simple—if people see the amount of work that goes into creating ads, then such ads are unmasked for what they really are: images, rather than reflections of what's real.

Such unmasking is a key project of media literacy, which during the past two decades has become an increasingly critical project of feminism. Media literacy, simply put, is the ability to read, analyze, and contextualize information in a way that looks at its accuracy, its "framing," and where it comes from. A media-literate approach to watching a television commercial that featured, say, a young, white mother pitching dishwashing powder would involve questions such as, "What is this commercial selling? Who is the intended audience? What techniques—such as close-ups or word repetition—are being used?

What's Wrong with This Picture? Abortion in Pop Culture

In the summer of 2007, two movies were released on the subject of unwanted pregnancy. *Knocked Up* was a goofy mix of sweetness and raunch; *Waitress* was a plucky independent film whose plot mixed down-home truths with a dash of fantasy. But both movies had something in common: Neither could bring itself to use the word "abortion" to describe one option for its pregnant character. In *Knocked Up*, a mother referred to the process as "tak[ing] care of it" and a friend conjured "the word that rhymes with 'shmashmortion.'" In *Waitress*, the abusive husband of our unhappily married lass begs her not to "do the other thing." In the end, nobody has to worry about the A-word anymore—both women have the babies.

Knocked Up and *Waitress* served as a culmination of several decades in which abortion in popular culture has become both scarcer and more contentious. It seems odd that in a world in which TV and movie characters are regularly shown engaging in such extreme behavior as serial killing (*Dexter, Nip/Tuck*), self-castration (*Little Children*), and defecating on Flavor Flav's floor (*Flavor of Love*), something as reasonable—if heartbreaking—as terminating a pregnancy is still muffled with euphemisms and refusal.

Abortion, particularly on television, has always been a risky bet. Just after *Roe v. Wade* made abortion legal in 1973, television saw its first

What would be different about this commercial if the person were a Latina, or a white man?" Media literacy is often employed to look at how race, class, and political views are prioritized—or denigrated—in popular culture or to look at how certain products—cigarettes, for instance—are specifically marketed to specific demographics. Let's say a prime-time TV sitcom features a teenage female character who gets pregnant and decides to have an abortion; on the next episode, she dies in a fiery car crash. You do a little digging into the background of this episode and discover that originally, the car crash wasn't in the script.

two abortions—one on the soap opera *Another World*, the second on the sitcom *Maude*. Abortions as plot points cropped up throughout the 1980s as well, on shows such as hospital drama *St. Elsewhere* and female buddy-cop show *Cagney and Lacey*. But in the 1990s and 2000s, as abortion once again became a woman's most contested right, pop culture became ever more reluctant to present it straightforwardly.

There was the "ghost child" approach to abortion, in which a character has an abortion and is then haunted by a specter of the little lost soul, a predicament faced by two characters on *Six Feet Under*. Then there's the "hellfire and brimstone" approach, epitomized by a 2005 episode of the drama *Jack and Bobby* in which a character chooses, after much soul-searching, to have an abortion and almost immediately afterward is killed in the aforementioned car accident. Finally, there was the ever-popular "deus ex miscarriage" gambit, in which a character agonizes over whether or not to have an abortion—but is, in the end, conveniently relieved of the decision by losing the pregnancy in its early stages; this approach had its heyday in teen dramas of the 1990s, including *Dawson's Creek*, *Party of Five*, and *Beverly Hills, 90210*.

However studios, screenwriters, and networks choose to deal with abortion, it can't be ignored. Six million U.S. women become pregnant each year, and half of them don't intend to. Of those, almost half choose to terminate their pregnancies—and among those are a significant number who would say they oppose abortion. Given those numbers, is there really a persuasive reason that our pop culture shouldn't portray what for many women is simultaneously the best and the hardest decision they'll ever make?

A conservative religious group organized a letter-writing campaign to the TV network's biggest advertisers, threatening a boycott of those advertisers' products unless the advertisers told the network they would pull their sponsorship unless the episode were rewritten to condemn abortion. Hence the car crash of doom—not just a plot device but a moral statement handed down by someone who had nothing to do with the TV show's script. Media literacy is crucial to understanding the difference. (And by the way, the fiery-car-crash plot? True story.)

Americans receive an alarming number of media and pop culture messages, and there's real danger in simply absorbing them. Media literacy makes every consumer more responsible and more active; it may not make ads or movies or television shows any smarter or more creative, but if people (particularly the prized younger demographics advertisers yearn to snag) are aware of the machinations of media, they won't be poisoned by them. Along with media literacy comes the ongoing project of media and pop culture reform—making changes so that the media and pop culture we see actually reflects a picture of who's consuming it.

Thus, some of the most crucial intersections of feminism and pop culture these days come in the form of media literacy organizations. Some of these groups focus specifically on media's messages to women and girls, such as About-Face, Women in Media and News, Dads and Daughters, and the long-running quarterly journal *Media Report to Women*. Others focus on teaching young viewers critical-thinking skills, such as Just Think and Children's Media Project, or ferreting out information on corporate influence on the media, such as Well Connected.

More media and pop culture exists now than at any other time in American history. It's not a good thing or a bad thing; it just is. And pop culture has more and more come to define us. It the main lens through which we look to understand ourselves and those around us: It helps us decide who we are, who our friends are, and who we want to be. It tells us what clothes to wear if we want to look cool, what car to drive if we want to be successful, and how to treat those who are different from us in race or class or creed. It tells us whom we should date and how we should expect to be treated; it tells us of whom and of what we should be scared, and what should make us happy. Anything pop culture can tell us, it will.

There's more. Politics, once considered far more serious and rarefied than mere pop culture, has itself *become* pop culture. Twenty years ago, it would have been unthinkable for a presidential candidate, say, to park his or her butt on the couch at *The Tonight Show* or *Late Night with David Letterman*. These days, it's necessary. Twenty years ago, we weren't supposed to want to sit down for a beer with our commander-in-chief; today, a poll question such as "Which candidate would you rather share a beer with?" is the kind of question that can literally influence election outcomes. Twenty years ago, we wanted to elect politicians who were smart—far smarter than we were. These days, we worry if our elected officials seem too smart.

We hear repeatedly that American culture has been lowest-common-denominated, that we as a society are getting more stupid because our culture is getting more stupid. Though there is always a clutch of optimistic intellectuals who say that, in fact, more complex television plot arcs and more intricate, strategy-based video games serve to actually sharpen our problem-solving and reasoning skills, an equal number see a future that looks a lot like a 2006 movie called *Idiocracy*; the plot, set in the year 2505, centers around a populace that has become so mentally poisoned by pop culture noise that it can barely function. (The film makes frequent reference to a TV show called *Ow! My Balls!*—which, chillingly, is not unlike two shows that already exist, one called *Holy %&!#$* and another called *Scarred*.) There are arguments to be made for both sides, and which are beyond the scope of this book, but looking around makes it easy to be very worried that the more media and pop culture there is, the less any of it seems to make sense.

The 1990s ushered in a time of frenzied media consolidation. Government deregulation of media ownership allowed for escalating media monopolies wherein it was entirely conceivable that a city's newspapers, cable TV system, and radio and TV station could all be owned by one company—a situation that was once unthinkable on the grounds that unbiased media serve the public's interest. On a national level, it didn't take long before nearly every major movie studio, TV network, magazine publisher, book imprint, and record label was owned by one of just a handful of multinational corporations, including Disney (which owns, among other things, ABC, ESPN, Pixar, and Miramax), Time Warner (*Time* and *People* magazines, HBO, CNN, AOL, the CW, and Rupert Murdoch's News Corp. (Fox networks,

Running in Place: Sexism, Media, and the Presidency

The idea that one day a woman might be elected to the highest office in the land has long been part of American women's slate of liberal-feminist hopes. Many women have, in fact, run for president: the early progressive Victoria Woodhull ran twice in the late 1800s, before women even had the right to vote; since then Shirley Chisholm, Leonora Fulani, and Elizabeth Dole have been among the women who set out on the campaign trail. Even pop culture has entertained the idea that a woman could run the country, on such TV shows as *24*, which in the 2008 season featured a female U.S. president, and the short-lived *Commander in Chief*, which featured Geena Davis as the titular character.

So when U.S. senator and former first lady Hillary Clinton began her campaign for the presidency in 2007, many women were elated at the thought of seeing a nonfictional female president. But as much as Clinton's journey was a potential inspiration in the realm of women and party politics, it was also a sobering illustration of the mainstream media's limited vision of women's power.

A slew of pointed, petty criticisms of Clinton began even before the ink on her campaign posters had dried. News commentators and journalists

20th Century Fox studios, HarperCollins, DirecTV, the *New York Post,* MySpace). And the Federal Communications Commission, the government body that regulates media ownership, continues to allow media conglomerates to buy up ever more local and national media properties.

The intent of media conglomeration may not be to silence independent voices, but that is undeniably one of its effects. These companies are driven exclusively by the bottom line, and they are most interested in producing content that appeals to their advertisers' target demographics. Their firm grip on the means of production also ensures that independent media owners—for instance, a radio station devoted to progressive hip-hop, or a cable TV network developed by and for pilloried her for her laugh (promptly dubbed a "cackle") and for the perceived crime of showing a half-inch of cleavage at a public appearance. They endlessly analyzed her "emotional moment" in New Hampshire, when she teared up as she spoke about her motivation for putting herself through the demands of the campaign trail. The most egregious of the sexism came, unsurprisingly, from right-wing mouthpieces like radio host Rush Limbaugh, who made repeated references to Clinton's "testicle lockbox," likened her to both a nagging housewife and the sadistic Nurse Ratched, and claimed that the American people wouldn't stand to watch a woman age in public. Fellow blowhard Tucker Carlson joked that he felt compelled to cross his legs every time Clinton opened her mouth. (This Clinton-related castration anxiety eventually led some wag to market a "Hillary nutcracker"—"with stainless steel thighs!") But even journalists and commentators whose careers aren't devoted to bashing Democrats seemed happy to join in the pile-on. "Shrill," "strident," "bitch," even "cunt"—all were tossed around as descriptors for the candidate. But for what seemed like a majority of these mudslingers, Clinton's stand on actual political issues wasn't their problem with her. Politics has always been an ugly, unforgiving game, and Clinton, like any candidate, is far from perfect. The undeniably sexist treatment of Clinton during the primaries may prove to be, troublingly, the most indelible legacy of her failed bid for the White House.

gay people—have little chance at success. Simply put, what's great for big media conglomerates is terrible for media diversity, and the entities that once claimed to serve the people now serve only the bankbooks of a few massive corporations that simply don't care about producing content by and for a diverse range of people, including women.

What this means is that, now more than ever, pop culture must be a locus of feminism and feminist activism. Is pop culture frivolous? Sure, sometimes. Are ad campaigns just soulless efforts to get you to part with your cash on behalf of the beauty-industrial complex? You bet. And are newspapers and magazines just trying to scare women with articles on everything from increasing rates of cervical cancer to plummeting rates of marriage for working women? Indeed. But that's all the more reason to keep an eye on them. You've heard the phrase "marketplace of ideas"? That's pop culture, quite literally, and people who don't engage with it risk having no voice in how it represents them. Consider this perspective, from the writer Angela Johnson in a 1994 issue of feminist journal *off our backs*:

> *I spent the first few years of my adulthood rigorously rejecting all mainstream culture. . . . I lost track, in a most delightful way, of what was hot—no TV, no radio, no magazines, just feminist lectures and lesbian parties, stimulating and bracing. . . . But slowly, something happened, and I found myself creeping down to watch* Dynasty *on the dorm TV. It was Steve and Luke that did it—it was a political act to watch their relationship unfold; but, you know, before they'd broken up I was hooked. Soon I was following Madonna— again a political act; this brazen woman, flaunting her round belly—she excited me as a symbol of female independence. By the time she was going around labeling herself Boy toy—hooked again. And I don't want you to think these things supplanted the ardent discussions of body hair and intersecting oppressions; they didn't. . . . [H]owever, they are part of me, whether I like it or not.*

You could substitute any of the characters on *The L Word* or *Queer as Folk* for "Steve and Luke," swap in Beyoncé's bootylicious body for Madonna's round belly, and have a picture of why pop culture today is no less alluring for viewers such as Johnson. Pop culture is as complicated, frustrating, and full of mixed signals for women as it's ever been. It's imperative that feminists continue to analyze it, create it, critique it—and ultimately, make it better.

READER'S GUIDE

Questions for Discussion

Has popular culture had an influence on how you view the differences between women and men? How?

Has popular culture influenced how you understand race and class? In what way?

When you see something in a TV show or movie that seems sexist to you, do you point it out or discuss it with friends or family? Why or why not?

What are the first associations that come to mind when you hear the word "feminist"? Where have those associations come from?

What would you do to improve the pop culture around you? What would you add? What would you take away? What would you prioritize?

Topics for Research

Representation of Women and Girls

Watch two to four hours of television in one day with an eye toward what women and girls are doing on screen. What roles do they have? What responsibilities? How do race and class play into these representations? Are women portrayed as different from men? What are shown to be their crucial concerns? Are they represented in television shows differently from how they are presented in commercials?

Representation of Alternative Sexualities

How have gay, lesbian, bisexual, and transgender characterizations evolved in pop culture through time? How do such portrayals in television now differ from those ten or twenty years ago?

Media Literacy

Research your favorite TV show, magazine, or movie. What is its overarching message? Who wrote, produced, edited it? Are there women involved in its creation? Who is its parent company, and what else does it own? Who are its advertisers? Do these things ultimately influence the vision and point of view of the final product?

Coverage of Women in Politics

Collect several articles on prominent women in politics. Compare them with similar articles on men. Is there a difference in the way the articles talk about the politicians? If so, what are these differences?

Pop Culture Created by Women

Research and look at movies, television, and magazines made by women. What are some common themes? How are women portrayed? Do their characterizations seem different from those in pop culture created by men? How so?

FURTHER READING AND RESOURCES

BOOKS
Feminism and Popular Culture, General

Antler, Joyce, ed. *Talking Back: Images of Jewish Women in American Popular Culture.* Hanover, NH: University Press of New England, 1998.

Bonner, Frances, et al., eds. *Imagining Women: Cultural Representations and Gender.* Oxford: Blackwell, 1992.

Bradley, Patricia. *Mass Media and the Shaping of American Feminism, 1963–1975.* Jackson: University Press of Mississippi, 2003.

Browne, Ray B., ed. *Profiles of Popular Culture: A Reader.* Madison: Popular Press/University of Wisconsin Press, 2005.

Buszek, Maria Elena. *Pin-up Grrrls: Feminism, Sexuality, Popular Culture.* Durham, NC: Duke University Press, 2006.

Carter, Cynthia, and Linda Steiner. *Critical Readings: Media and Gender.* Maidenhed, Berkshire UK: Open University Press, 2003.

Creekmur, Corey K., and Alexander Doty, eds. *Out in Culture: Gay, Lesbian, and Queer Essays on Popular Culture.* Durham, NC: Duke University Press, 1995.

Dines, Gail, and Jean M. Humez, eds. *Gender, Race, and Class in Media A Text Reader.* Thousand Oaks, CA: Sage, 2002.

Douglas, Susan J. *Where the Girls Are: Growing Up Female with the Mass Media.* New York: Times Books, 1994.

Early, Frances, and Kathleen Kennedy, eds. *Athena's Daughters: Television's New Women Warriors.* Syracuse, NY: Syracuse University Press, 2003.

Fiske, John. *Reading the Popular.* New York: Routledge, 1989.

———. *Understanding Popular Culture.* New York: Routledge, 1989.

Freccero, Carla. *Popular Culture: An Introduction.* New York: New York University Press, 1999.

Gauntlett, David. *Media, Gender and Identity: An Introduction.* New York: Routledge, 2002.

Guerrilla Girls. *Bitches, Bimbos, and Ballbreakers: The Guerrilla Girls' Illustrated Guide to Female Stereotypes.* New York: Penguin, 2003.

Habell-Pallán, Michelle, and Mary Romero, eds. *Latino/a Popular Culture*. New York: New York University Press, 2002.

Hamer, Diane, and Belinda Budge, eds. *The Good, the Bad and the Gorgeous: Popular Culture's Romance with Lesbianism*. New York: New York University Press, 1994.

Hermes, Joke. *Re-Reading Popular Culture: Rethinking Gender, Television, and Popular Media Audiences*. Oxford: Blackwell, 2005.

Heywood, Leslie, and Jennifer Drake, eds. *Third Wave Agenda: Being Feminist, Doing Feminism*. Minneapolis: University of Minnesota Press, 1997.

Hinds, Harold E., Marilyn F. Motz, and Angela M. S. Nelson, eds. *Popular Culture Theory and Methodology: A Basic Introduction*. Madison: Popular Press/University of Wisconsin Press, 2006.

Hobson, Janell. *Venus in the Dark: Blackness and Beauty in Popular Culture*. New York: Routledge, 2005.

Hollows, Joanne. *Feminism, Femininity and Popular Culture*. Manchester, UK: Manchester University Press, 2000.

Hollows, Joanne, and Rachel Moseley, eds. *Feminism in Popular Culture*. Oxford: Berg, 2006.

Holmberg, Carl B. *Sexualities and Popular Culture*. Thousand Oaks, CA: Sage, 1998.

hooks, bell. *Black Looks: Race and Representation*. Boston: South End Press, 1992.

Inness, Sherrie A. *Tough Girls: Women Warriors and Wonder Women in Popular Culture*. Philadelphia: University of Pennsylvania Press, 1998

———, ed. *Disco Divas: Women and Popular Culture in the 1970s*. Philadelphia: University of Pennsylvania Press, 2003.

———, ed. *Action Chicks: New Images of Tough Women in Popular Culture*. New York: Palgrave McMillan, 2004.

———, ed. *Geek Chic: Smart Women in Popular Culture*. New York: Palgrave MacMillan, 2007.

Jackson, Sandra, and Ann Russo, eds. *Talking Back and Acting Out: Women Negotiating the Media Across Culture*. New York: Peter Lang, 2002.

Johnson, Merri Lisa, ed. *Third Wave Feminism and Television: Jane Puts It in a Box*. London: I. B. Tauris, 2007.

Jones, Amelia, ed. *The Feminism and Visual Culture Reader*. New York: Routledge, 2002.

Kruger, Barbara. *Remote Control: Power, Cultures, and the World of Appearances*. Cambridge, MA: MIT Press, 1994.

Macdonald, Myra. *Representing Women: Myths of Femininity in the Popular Media*. London: Hodder Arnold, 1995.

McCaughey, Martha, and Neal King, eds. *Reel Knockouts: Violent Women in the Movies*. Austin: University of Texas Press, 2001.

Meyers, Marian, ed. *Mediated Women: Representations in Popular Culture*. Cresskill, NJ: Hampton Press, 1999.

Miklitsch, Robert. *Roll Over Adorno: Critical Theory, Popular Culture, Audiovisual Media*. Albany: State University of New York Press, 2006.

Modleski, Tania, ed. *Studies in Entertainment: Critical Approaches to Mass Culture.* Bloomington: Indiana University Press, 1986.

Nash, Ilana. *American Sweethearts: Teenage Girls in Twentieth-Century Popular Culture.* Bloomington: Indiana University Press, 2006.

Rapping, Elayne. *Media-tions: Forays into the Culture and Gender Wars.* Boston: South End Press, 1994.

Raymond, Diane, ed. *Sexual Politics and Popular Culture.* Bowling Green, OH: Bowling Green State University Popular Press, 1990.

Robertson, Pamela. *Guilty Pleasures: Feminist Camp from Mae West to Madonna.* London: I. B. Tauris, 1996.

Robinson, Lillian S. *Wonder Women: Feminisms and Superheroes.* New York: Routledge, 2004.

Ross, Andrew. *No Respect: Intellectuals and Pop Culture.* New York: Routledge, 1989.

Schwichtenberg, Cathy, ed. *The Madonna Connection: Representational Politics, Subcultural Identities, and Cultural Theory.* Boulder, CO: Westview Press, 1993.

Shiach, Morag, ed. *Feminism and Cultural Studies.* New York: Oxford University Press, 1999.

Storey, John. *Cultural Studies and the Study of Popular Culture: Theories and Methods.* 2nd ed. Athens: University of Georgia Press, 2003.

———, ed. *Cultural Theory and Popular Culture: A Reader.* 3rd ed. Athens: University of Georgia Press, 2006.

Thomas, Lyn. *Fans, Feminisms and Quality Media.* New York: Routledge, 2002.

Valdivia, Angharad N. *A Latina in the Land of Hollywood and Other Essays on Media Culture.* Tucson: University of Arizona Press, 2000.

Van Zoonen, Liesbet. *Feminist Media Studies.* Thousand Oaks, CA: Sage, 1994.

Walters, Suzanna, Danuta. *Material Girls: Making Sense of Feminist Cultural Theory.* Berkeley: University of California Press, 1995.

Watson, Elwood, and Darcy Martin, eds. *"There She Is, Miss America": The Politics of Sex, Beauty, and Race in America's Most Famous Pageant.* New York: Palgrave MacMillan, 2004.

Whelehan, Imelda. *Overloaded: Popular Culture and the Future of Feminism.* London: Women's Press, 2000.

Williamson, Judith. *Consuming Passions: The Dynamics of Popular Culture.* London: Marion Boyars, 1986.

Film and Spectatorship

Carson, Diane, Linda Dittmar, and Janice R. Welsch, eds. *Multiple Voices in Feminist Film Criticism.* Minneapolis: University of Minnesota Press, 1994.

Clover, Carol J. *Men, Women and Chain Saws: Gender in the Modern Horror Film.* Princeton, NJ: Princeton University Press, 1992.

Cook, Pam, and Philip Dodd, eds. *Women and Film: A Sight and Sound Reader.* Philadelphia: Temple University Press, 1993.

Creed, Barbara. *The Monstrous-Feminine: Film, Feminism, Psychoanalysis.* New York: Routledge, 1993.

de Lauretis, Teresa. *Alice Doesn't: Feminism, Semiotics, Cinema.* Bloomington: Indiana University Press, 1984.

———. *Technologies of Gender: Essays on Theory, Film, and Fiction.* Bloomington: Indiana University Press, 1987.

Doane, Mary Ann. *The Desire to Desire: The Woman's Film of the 1940s.* Bloomington: Indiana University Press, 1987.

———. *Femmes Fatales: Feminism, Film Theory, Psychoanalysis.* New York: Routledge, 1991.

Erens, Patricia, ed. *Issues in Feminist Film Criticism.* Bloomington: University of Indiana Press, 1991.

Fregoso, Rosa Linda. *The Bronze Screen: Chicana and Chicano Film Culture.* Minneapolis: University of Minnesota Press, 1993.

Gledhill, Christine. *Home Is Where the Heart Is: Studies in Melodrama and the Woman's Film.* London: British Film Institute, 1987.

Grant, Barry Keith, ed. *The Dread of Difference: Gender and the Horror Film.* Austin: University of Texas Press, 1996.

Haskell, Molly. *From Reverence to Rape: The Treatment of Women in the Movies.* 2nd ed. Chicago: University of Chicago Press, 1987.

Humm, Maggie. *Feminism and Film.* Bloomington: Indiana University Press, 1997.

Kaplan, E. Ann. *Women and Film: Both Sides of the Camera.* 1983. New York: Routledge, 2000.

———, ed. *Women in Film Noir.* Rev. ed. London: British Film Institute, 1998.

———, ed. *Feminism and Film.* Oxford and New York: Oxford University Press, 2000.

Kipnis, Laura. *Bound and Gagged: Pornography and the Politics of Fantasy in America.* Durham, NC: Duke University Press, 1999.

Lane, Christina. *Feminist Hollywood: From* Born from Flames *to* Point Break. Detroit: Wayne State University Press, 2000.

Mayne, Judith. *The Woman at the Keyhole: Feminism and Women's Cinema.* Bloomington: Indiana University Press, 1990.

———. *Cinema and Spectatorship.* New York: Routledge, 1993.

Modleski, Tania. *The Women Who Knew Too Much: Hitchcock and Feminist Theory.* London: Methuen, 1988.

Mulvey, Laura. "Visual Pleasure and Narrative Cinema." *Screen* 16.3, 1975.

Penley, Constance, ed. *Feminism and Film Theory.* New York: Routledge, 1988.

Petro, Patrice. *Aftershocks of the New: Feminism and Film History.* Piscataway, NJ: Rutgers University Press, 2002.

Redding, Judith M., and Victoria A. Brownworth. *Film Fatales: Independent Women Directors.* Seattle: Seal, 1997.

Rich, B. Ruby. *Chick Flicks: Theories and Memories of the Feminist Film Movement.* Durham, NC: Duke University Press, 1998.

Silverman, Kaja. *The Acoustic Mirror: The Female Voice in Psychoanalysis and Cinema.* Bloomington: Indiana University Press, 1988.

Svehla, Gary J., and Susan Svehla, eds. *Bitches, Bimbos, and Virgins: Women in the Horror Film.* Baltimore: Midnight Marquee Press, 1996.

Thornham, Sue, ed. *Feminist Film Theory: A Reader*. New York: New York University Press, 1999.

Weiss, Andrea. *Vampires and Violets: Lesbians in Film*. New York: Penguin, 1993.

White, Patricia. *Uninvited: Classical Hollywood Cinema and Lesbian Representability*. Bloomington: Indiana University Press, 1999.

TV

Akass, Kim, and Janet McCabe, eds. *Reading Sex and the City*. London: I. B. Tauris, 2004.

Akass, Kim, and Janet McCabe, eds. *Reading The L Word: Outing Contemporary Television*. London: I. B. Tauris, 2006.

Allen, Robert C., ed. *Channels of Discourse, Reassembled: Television and Contemporary Criticism*. 2nd ed. Chapel Hill: University of North Carolina Press, 1992.

Andrejevic, Mark. *Reality TV; The Work of Being Watched*. Lanham, MD: Rowman & Littlefield, 2003.

Ang, Ien. *Watching Dallas: Soap Opera and the Melodramatic Imagination*. New York: Routledge, 1985.

Baehr, Helen, and Ann Gray, eds. *Turning It On: A Reader in Women and Media*. London: Hodder Arnold, 1995.

Brown, Mary Ellen, ed. *Television and Women's Culture: The Politics of the Popular*. Thousand Oaks, CA: Sage, 1990.

———. *Soap Opera and Women's Talk: The Pleasure of Resistance*. Thousand Oaks, CA: Sage, 1994.

Brunsdon, Charlotte. *The Feminist, The Housewife, and the Soap Opera*. New York: Oxford University Press, 2000.

Brunsdon, Charlotte, Julie D'Acci, and Lynn Spigel, eds. *Feminist Television Criticism: A Reader*. New York: Oxford University Press, 1997.

Carter, Cynthia. *News, Gender and Power*. New York: Routledge, 1998.

Dow, Bonnie J. *Prime-Time Feminism: Television, Media Culture, and the Women's Movement Since 1970*. Philadelphia: University of Pennsylvania Press, 1996.

Feuer, Jane. *Seeing Through the Eighties: Television and Reaganism*. Durham, NC: Duke University Press, 1995.

Fiske, John. *Television Culture*. New York: Routledge, 1989.

Haralovich, Mary Beth, and Lauren Rabinovitz, eds. *Television, History, and American Culture: Feminist Critical Essays*. Durham, NC: Duke University Press, 1999.

Heide, Margaret J. *Television Culture and Women's Lives: Thirtysomething and the Contradictions of Gender*. Philadelphia: University of Pennsylvania Press, 1995.

Heller, Dana, ed. *Makeover Television: Realities Remodelled*. London: I. B. Tauris, 2007.

Hermes, Joke. *Re-Reading Popular Culture: Rethinking Gender, Television, and Popular, Media Audiences*. Oxford: Blackwell, 2005.

Holmes, Su, and Deborah Jermyn, eds. *Understanding Reality Television*. New York: Routledge, 2004.

Jowett, Lorna. *Sex and the Slayer: A Gender Studies Primer for the Buffy Fan*. Middleton, CT: Wesleyan University Press, 2005.

Kaplan, E. Ann, ed. *Regarding Television: Critical Approaches—An Anthology.* Frederick MD: University of America Press, 1983.

———. *Rocking Around the Clock: Music Television, Postmodernism, and Consumer Culture.* New York: Routledge, 1987.

Klein, Allison. *What Would Murphy Brown Do?: How the Women of Prime Time Changed Our Lives.* Berkeley, CA: Seal, 2006.

Lewis, Lisa A. *Gender Politics and MTV: Voicing the Difference.* Philadelphia: Temple University Press, 1991.

Lotz, Amanda D. *Redesigning Women: Television After the Network Era.* Champaign-Urbana: University of Illinois Press, 2006.

McCabe, Janet, and Kim Akass, eds. *Reading* Desperate Housewives: *Beyond the White Picket Fence.* London: I. B. Tauris, 2006.

Mellencamp, Patricia, ed. *Logics of Television: Essays in Cultural Criticism.* Bloomington: Indiana University Press, 1990.

Nochimson, Martha. *No End to Her: Soap Opera and the Female Subject.* Berkeley: University of California Press, 1993.

Press, Andrea L. *Women Watching Television: Gender, Class, and Generation in the American Television Experience.* Philadelphia: University of Pennsylvania Press, 1991.

Projansky, Sarah. *Watching Rape: Film and Television in Postfeminist Culture.* New York: New York University Press, 2001.

Rapping, Elayne. *The Movie of the Week: Private Stories/Public Events.* Minneapolis: University of Minnesota Press, 1992.

Shattuc, Jane M. *The Talking Cure: TV Talk Shows and Women.* New York: Routledge, 1997.

Smith-Shomade, Beretta E. *Shaded Lives: African-American Women and Television.* Piscataway, NJ: Rutgers University Press, 2002.

Spigel, Lynn. *Make Room for TV: Television and the Family Ideal in Postwar America.* Chicago: University of Chicago Press, 1992.

Spigel, Lynn, and Denise Mann, eds. *Private Screenings: Television and the Female Consumer.* Minneapolis: University of Minnesota Press, 1992.

Advertising and Consumer Culture

Barthel, Diane. *Putting on Appearances: Gender and Advertising.* Philadelphia: Temple University Press, 1989.

Cortese, Anthony J. *Provocateur: Images of Women and Minorities in Advertising.* 3rd ed. Lanham, MD: Rowman & Littlefield, 2007.

Costa, Janeen Arnold, ed. *Gender Issues and Consumer Behavior.* Thousand Oaks, CA: Sage, 1994.

Ewen, Stuart. *Captains of Consciousness: Advertising and the Social Roots of the Consumer Culture.* 1976. New York: Basic Books, 2001.

Fowles, Jib. *Advertising and Popular Culture.* Thousand Oaks, CA: Sage, 1996.

Jhally, Sut. *The Codes of Advertising: Fetishism and the Political Economy of Meaning in the Consumer Society.* New York: St. Martin's Press, 1987.

Kilbourne, Jean. *Can't Buy My Love: How Advertising Changes the Way We Think and Feel.* New York: Free Press, 2000.

Peiss, Kathy. *Hope in a Jar: The Making of America's Beauty Culture.* New York: Metropolitan Books, 1998.

Wolf, Naomi. *The Beauty Myth: How Images of Beauty Are Used Against Women.* 1991. New York: HarperCollins, 2002.

Women Readers

Loudermilk, Kim A. *Fictional Feminism: How American Bestsellers Affect the Movement for Women's Equality.* New York: Routledge, 2004.

Makinen, Merja. *Feminist Popular Fiction.* New York: Palgrave, 2001.

Modleski, Tania. *Loving with a Vengeance: Mass-Produced Fantasies for Women.* 1982. 2nd ed. New York: Routledge, 2007.

Radway, Janice A. *Reading the Romance: Women, Patriarchy, and Popular Literature.* Chapel Hill: University of North Carolina Press, 1991.

Magazines

Beetham, Margaret, et al. *Women's Worlds: Ideology, Femininity and the Woman's Magazine.* New York: New York University Press, 1992.

Duncombe, Stephen. *Notes from Underground: Zines and the Politics of Alternative Culture.* New York and London: Verso, 1997.

Farrell, Amy Erdman. *Yours in Sisterhood: Ms. Magazine and the Promise of Popular Feminism.* Chapel Hill: The University of North Carolina Press, 1998.

Gough-Yates, Ann. *Understanding Women's Magazines: Publishing, Markets and Readerships.* New York: Routledge, 2003.

Green, Karen, and Tristan Taormino. *A Girl's Guide to Taking Over the World: Writings from the Girl Zine Revolution.* New York: St. Martin's Griffin, 1997.

Hermes, Joke. *Reading Women's Magazines: An Analysis of Everyday Media Use.* Cambridge: Polity Press, 1996.

Jervis, Lisa, and Andi Zeisler, eds. *BITCHfest: Ten Years of Cultural Criticism from the Pages of Bitch Magazine.* New York: Farrar, Straus & Giroux, 2006.

Jesella, Kara, and Marisa Meltzer. *How Sassy Changed My Life: A Love Letter to the Greatest Teen Magazine of All Time.* New York: Faber and Faber, 2007.

Karp, Marcelle, and Debbie Stoller, eds. *The Bust Guide to the New Girl Order.* New York: Penguin, 1999.

Kipnis, Laura. "(Male) Desire and (Female) Disgust: Reading *Hustler.*" In *Cultural Studies* edited by Lawrence Grossberg, Cary Nelson, and Paula Treichler. 373-91. New York: Routledge, 1992.

Kitch, Carolyn. *The Girl on the Magazine Cover: The Origins of Visual Stereotypes in American Mass Media.* Chapel Hill: The University of North Carolina Press, 2000.

Robbins, Trina. *From Girls to Grrlz: A History of Women's Comics from Teens to Zines.* San Francisco: Chronicle Books, 1999.

Rooks, Noliwe M. *Ladies' Pages: African American Women's Magazines and the Culture That Made Them.* New Brunswick, NJ: Rutgers University Press, 2004.

Thom, Mary. *Inside Ms.: 25 Years of the Magazine and the Feminist Movement.* New York: Henry Holt & Co., 1997.

Todd, Mark, and Esther Pearl, Watson. *Whatcha Mean, What's a Zine?* New York: Graphia, 2006.

Vale, V. *ZINES! Incendiary Interviews with Independent Publishers.* 2 vols. San Francisco: Re/Search, 1997.

Walker, Nancy A., ed. *Women's Magazines, 1940–1960: Gender Roles and the Popular Press.* New York: Palgrave Macmillan, 1998.

Zuckerman, Mary Ellen. *A History of Popular Women's Magazines in the United States, 1792–1995.* Westport, CT: Greenwood Press, 1998.

Music

Ammer, Christine. *Unsung: A History of Women in American Music.* 2nd ed. New York: Amadeus Press, 2001.

Aparicio, Frances R. *Listening to Salsa: Gender, Latin Popular Music, and Puerto Rican Cultures.* Hanover, NH: University Press of New England, 1998.

Burns, Lori, and Mélisse LaFrance. *Disruptive Divas: Feminism, Identity and Popular Music.* New York: Routledge, 2002.

Carson, Mina, see queries for et al., *Girls Rock!: Fifty Years of Women Making Music.* Lexington: University Press of Kentucky, 2004.

Collins, Patricia Hill. *From Black Power to Hip Hop: Racism, Nationalism, and Feminism.* Philadelphia: Temple University Press, 2006.

Davis, Angela Y. *Blues Legacies and Black Feminism: Gertrude "Ma" Rainey, Bessie Smith, and Billie Holiday.* New York: Pantheon, 1998.

Gaar, Gillian G. *She's a Rebel: The History of Women in Rock and Roll.* 2nd ed. Berkeley, CA: Seal, 2002.

Hirshey, Gerri. *We Gotta Get Out of This Place: The True, Tough Story of Women in Rock.* New York: Atlantic, 2001.

Leblanc, Lauraine. *Pretty in Punk: Girls' Gender Resistance in a Boys' Subculture.* New Brunswick NJ: Rutgers University Press, 1999.

Marcic, Dorothy. *Respect: Women and Popular Music.* New York: Texere, 2002.

Morgan, Joan. *When Chickenheads Come Home to Roost: A Hip-Hop Feminist Breaks It Down.* New York: Simon & Schuster, 2000.

O'Brien, Lucy. *She Bop: The Definitive History of Women in Rock, Pop & Soul.* New York: Penguin, 1996.

———. *She Bop II: The Definitive History of Women in Rock, Pop and Soul.* New York: Continuum, 2004.

Pendle, Karin ed. *Women and Music: A History.* 2nd ed. Bloomington: Indiana University Press, 2001.

Pough, Gwendolyn D. *Check It While I Wreck It: Black Womanhood, Hip Hop Culture, and the Public Sphere*. see queries New England: Northeastern University Press, 2004.

Pough, Gwendolyn D., et al., eds. *Home Girls Make Some Noise!: Hip Hop Feminism Anthology*. Mira Loma, CA: Parker, 2007.

Raha, Maria. *Cinderella's Big Score: Women of the Punk and Indie Underground*. Berkeley, CA: Seal, 2005.

Reynolds, Simon, and Joy Press. *The Sex Revolts: Gender, Rebellion, and Rock 'n' Roll*. Cambridge, MA: Harvard University Press, 1995, 2006.

Rhodes, Lisa L. *Electric Ladyland: Women and Rock Culture*. Philadelphia: University of Pennsylvania Press, 2005.

Riley, Tim. *Fever: How Rock 'n' Roll Transformed Gender in America*. New York: St. Martin's, 2004; Picador, 2005.

Rose, Tricia. *Black Noise: Rap Music and Black Culture in Contemporary America*. Hanover, NH: University Press of New England/Wesleyan University Press, 1994.

Savage, Ann M. *They're Playing Our Songs: Women Talk About Feminist Rock Music*. Westport, CT: Praeger, 2003.

Schippers, Mimi. *Rockin' out of the Box: Gender Maneuvering in Alternative Hard Rock*. New Brunswick NJ: Rutgers University Press, 2002.

Sharpley-Whiting, T. Denean. *Pimps Up, Ho's Down: Hip Hop's Hold on Young Black Women*. New York: New York University Press, 2007.

Whiteley, Sheila, ed. *Sexing the Groove: Popular Music and Gender*. New York: Routledge, 1997.

———*Women and Popular Music: Sexuality, Identity and Subjectivity*. New York: Routledge, 2000.

JOURNALS

Americana: The Journal of American Popular Culture (1900–present). Published by The Institute for the Study of American Popular Culture: www.americanpopularculture.com/journal/index.htm

Camera Obscura. A journal of feminist perspectives on film, television, and visual media. Published by Duke University Press: www.dukeupress.edu/cameraobscura

differences: A Journal of Feminist Cultural Studies. Published by Duke University Press: www.dukeupress.edu/differences

The Journal of Popular Culture. The official publication of the Pop Culture Association. Published by Blackwell: www.msu.edu/~tjpc

Screen. The foremost international journal of film and television studies. Published by the University of Glasgow: www.screen.arts.gla.ac.uk

Signs: Journal of Women in Culture and Society. Published by the University of Chicago Press: www.journals.uchicago.edu/Signs

FILMS

Don't Need You: The Herstory of Riot Grrrl. Directed by Kerri Koch. Urban Cowgirl, 2006.

Dreamworlds: Gender/Sex/Power in Rock Video (1990); *Dreamworlds II: Gender/Sex/Power in Music Video* (1995); *Dreamworlds 3: Gender/Sex/Power in Music Video* (2007). Directed by Sut Jhally. Media Education Foundation.

Girls Rock! Directed by Arne Johnson and Shane King. Girls Rock Productions, 2007.

Grrlyshow. Directed by Kara Herold. Women Make Movies, 2000.

Iron Jawed Angels. Directed by Katja von Garnier. HBO Films, 2004.

Killing Us Softly (1979); *Still Killing Us Softly* (1987); *Killing Us Softly 3* (2000). Created by Jean Kilbourne. Media Education Foundation.

Sisters of '77. Directed by Cynthia Salzman Mondell and Allen Mondell. Circle R Media, LLC, and Media Projects, Inc., 2005.

WEBSITES

About-Face: www.about-face.org

Americana: The Institute for the Study of American Popular Culture: www.american popularculture.com

Bitch: Feminist Response to Pop Culture: www.bitchmagazine.org

Blogging in College: The Gender & Pop Culture Blog Experiment: http://genderpop culture.blogspot.com

Feministing: www.feministing.com

Femtique: Feminist Critique of Pop Media: www.femtique.net

Guerrilla Girls: www.guerrillagirls.com

The Hathor Legacy: The Search for Good Female Characters: http://thehathorlegacy.info

Images: A Journal of Film and Popular Culture: www.imagesjournal.com

Mediagirl.org: www.mediagirl.org

Pop Culture Heroines: Strong Female Characters in Popular Culture: http://popculture heroines.com

Popcultures.com: www.popcultures.com

Pop Matters: www.popmatters.com

PopPolitics.com: Where Popular and Political Cultures Meet: www.poppolitics.com

The Popular Culture Association/American Culture Association Page: http://pcaaca.org

Racialicious.com: The Intersection of Race and Pop Culture: www.racialicious.com

The Scholar and Feminist Online: www.barnard.columbia.edu/sfonline

WIMN's Voices: A Group Blog on Women, Media, and . . .: www.wimnonline.org /WIMNsVoicesBlog

SOURCES

Chapter 1

Benjamin, Walter. "The Work of Art in the Age of Mechanical Reproduction." 1936. In Walter Benjamin, *Illuminations: Essays and Reflections*. New York: Schocken, 1969, pp. 217–252.

Berger, John. *Ways of Seeing*. London: British Broadcasting Company and Penguin Books, 1972, p. 47.

Brownmiller, Susan. *Femininity*. New York: Ballantine Books, 1985, p. 51.

Douglas, Susan J. *Where the Girls Are: Growing Up Female with the Mass Media*. New York: Times Books, 1994, p. 10.

Dowd, Maureen. *Are Men Necessary? When Sexes Collide*. New York: Putnam, 2005.

Falwell, Jerry. *The 700 Club*. (CBN), September 13, 2001.

Finke, Nikki, "Hollywood's He-Man Woman Haters Club." *L.A. Weekly*, Wednesday, October 17, 2007.

Levy, Ariel. *Female Chauvinist Pigs: Women and the Rise of Raunch Culture*. New York: Free Press, 2005, pp. 89–91.

McGinn, Daniel. "Marriage by the Numbers." *Newsweek*, June 5, 2006.

Mulvey, Laura, "Visual Pleasure and Narrative Cinema." *Screen* 16.3, 1975. In Laura Mulvey, *Visual and Other Pleasures*. Bloomington: Indiana University Press, 1989.

Reed, Jennifer. "Roseanne: A 'Killer Bitch' for Generation X." In Leslie Heywood and Jennifer Drake, eds. *Third Wave Agenda: Being Feminist, Doing Feminism*. Minneapolis: University of Minnesota Press, 1997, p. 123.

"Robertson Letter Attacks Feminists." *New York Times*, August 26, 1992.

Thompson, Anne. "Warner Bros. Still Committed to Women." Variety.com, October 9, 2007.

"Too Late for Prince Charming?" *Newsweek*, June 2, 1986.

Chapter 2

Brownmiller, Susan. *In Our Time: Memoir of a Revolution*. New York: Dial, 1999, pp. 35–41, 83–92.

Buszek, Maria Elena. *Pin-Up Grrrls: Feminism, Sexuality, Popular Culture*. Durham, NC: Duke University Press, 2006, p. 213.

Coontz, Stephanie, *The Way We Never Were: America's Families and the Nostalgia Trap*. New York: Basic Books, 1992, p. 9.

Des Barres, Pamela. *I'm with the Band: Confessions of a Groupie*. New York: Beech Tree Books/William Morrow, 1987, p. 29.

Douglas, Susan J. *Where the Girls Are: Growing Up Female with the Mass Media*. New York: Times Books, 1994, pp. 50, 83–98.

Douglas, Susan J., and Meredith W. Michaels. *The Mommy Myth: The Idealization of Motherhood and How It Has Undermined Women*. New York: Free Press, 2004.

Ehrenreich, Barbara, Elizabeth Hess, and Gloria Jacobs. "Beatlemania: Girls Just Want to Have Fun." In Lisa A. Lewis, ed., *The Adoring Audience: Fan Culture and Popular Media*. New York: Routledge, 1992, p. 85.

Friedan, Betty. *The Feminine Mystique*. New York: W. W. Norton & Company, 1963; rev. ed., 2001, p. xvi.

Haskell, Molly. *From Reverence to Rape: The Treatment of Women in the Movies*. New York: Holt, Rinehart & Winston, 1973, pp. 155–163.

Kilbourne, Jean. *Can't Buy My Love: How Advertising Changes the Way We Think and Feel*. New York: Free Press, 2000.

LaSalle, Mick. *Complicated Women: Power and Sex in Pre-Code Hollywood*. New York: Thomas Dunne Books, 2000, p. 1.

Morgan, Robin, ed. *Sisterhood Is Powerful: An Anthology of Writings from the Women's Liberation Movement*. New York: Random House, 1970, pp. 584–588.

O'Brien, Lucy. *She Bop II: The Definitive History of Women in Rock, Pop, and Soul*. New York: Continuum, 2004, pp. 75–78.

Reichert, Tom. *The Erotic History of Advertising*. New York: Prometheus Books, 2003, pp. 100–113.

Tay, Sharon Lin. "Constructing a Feminist Cinematic Genealogy: The Gothic Woman's Film Beyond Psychoanalysis." In *Women: A Cultural Review*, vol. 14, no. 3, 2003, pp. 265–271.

Van Gelder, Lindsy. "The Truth About Bra-Burners." *Ms.*, September/October 1992, pp. 80–81.

Chapter 3

Baumgardner, Jennifer, and Amy Richards. *Manifesta: Young Women, Feminism, and the Future*. New York: Farrar, Straus and Giroux, 2000, pp. 87–100, 116–119.

Brownmiller, Susan. *In Our Time: Memoir of a Revolution*. New York: Dial, 1999, pp. 136–151.

Clover, Carol J. *Men, Women, and Chain Saws: Gender in the Modern Horror Film*. Princeton, NJ: Princeton University Press, 1992.

Cole, Sheri Kathleen. "I Am the Eye, You Are My Victim: The Pornographic Ideology of Music Video." In *Enculturation*, vol. 2, no. 2, Spring 1999.

Davis, Kathy. *The Making of Our Bodies, Ourselves: How Feminism Travels Across Borders.* Durham, NC: Duke University Press, 2007.

Douglas, Susan J. *Where the Girls Are: Growing Up Female with the Mass Media.* New York: Times Books, 1994, pp. 194–201, 202–204.

Douglas, Susan J., and Meredith W. Michaels. *The Mommy Myth: The Idealization of Motherhood and How It Has Undermined Women.* New York: Free Press, 2004, pp. 60–61, 81–82.

Embree, Alice. "Media Images I: Madison Avenue Brainwashing—The Facts." In Robin Morgan, ed. *Sisterhood Is Powerful: An Anthology of Writings from the Women's Liberation Movement.* New York: Random House, 1970, pp. 194–212.

Faludi, Susan. *Backlash: The Undeclared War Against American Women.* New York: Anchor Books/Doubleday, 1991.

Farrell, Amy Erdman. *Yours in Sisterhood: Ms. Magazine and the Promise of Popular Feminism.* Chapel Hill, NC: University of North Carolina Press, 1998, p. 15

Freedman, Estelle B. *No Turning Back: The History of Feminism and the Future of Women.* New York: Ballantine Books, 2002.

Friedan, Betty. *The Feminine Mystique.* New York: W. W. Norton & Company, 1963; rev. ed., 2001.

Haskell, Molly. *From Reverence to Rape: The Treatment of Women in the Movies.* New York: Holt, Rinehart & Winston, 1973.

hooks, bell. "Madonna: Plantation Mistress or Soul Sister?" In *Black Looks: Race and Representation.* Boston: South End Press, 1992, pp. 157–64.

———. *Outlaw Culture: Resisting Representations.* New York: Routledge, 1994, pp. 16–26.

Kilbourne, Jean. *Can't Buy My Love: How Advertising Changes the Way We Think and Feel.* New York: Free Press, 2000.

Klein, Allison. *What Would Murphy Brown Do? How the Women of Prime Time Changed Our Lives.* Emeryville, CA: Seal, 2006, pp. 139–144.

Levine, Elana. *Wallowing in Sex: The New Sexual Culture of 1970s American Television.* Durham, NC: Duke University Press, 2007, pp. 136–142. [Emphasis in excerpt appears in original.]

Mainardi, Pat. "The Politics of Housework." In Robin Morgan, ed., *Sisterhood Is Powerful: An Anthology of Writings from the Women's Liberation Movement.* New York: Random House, 1970, pp. 501–510.

"Really Socking It to Women." *Time,* February 7, 1977.

Rhodes, Lisa L. *Electric Ladyland: Women and Rock Culture.* Philadelphia: University of Pennsylvania Press, 2005, pp. 137–149.

Spigel, Lynn. *Welcome to the Dreamhouse: Popular Media and Postwar Suburbs.* Durham, NC: Duke University Press, 2001.

Steinem, Gloria. "Sex, Lies and Advertising." *Ms.,* July 1990.

Thompson, Luke Y. Review, *I Spit on Your Grave,* posted February 4, 2003. RottenTomatoes.com.

Williams, Linda. "When the Woman Looks." In Barry Keith Grant, ed., *The Dread of Difference: Gender and the Horror Film*. Austin: University of Texas Press, 1996, pp. 15-34.

Willis, Ellen. "Women and the Myth of Consumerism." *Ramparts*, 1969.

Chapter 4

Bellafante, Ginia. "It's All About Me!" *Time*, June 29, 1998, pp. 54–60.

Brown, Janelle. "Is *Time* Brain-Dead?" *Salon*, June 25, 1998.

Cooper, Glenda, and Kate le Vann. "Is Ally McBeal a Nineties Heroine? Or a Grotesque Creation of Male Fantasy?" *The Independent*, November 8, 1998.

Douglas, Susan J. *Where the Girls Are: Growing Up Female with the Mass Media*. New York: Times Books, 1994, p. 285.

———. "Manufacturing Postfeminism." *In These Times*, May 13, 2002.

Dworkin, Susan. "Roseanne Barr: The Disgruntled Housewife as Stand-up Comedian." *Ms.* July-August 1987.

Faludi, Susan. *Backlash: The Undeclared War Against American Women*. New York: Anchor Books/Doubleday, 1991, pp. 112–123, 159–160.

Findlen, Barbara, ed. *Listen Up: Voices from the Next Feminist Generation*. Seattle: Seal, 1995.

Fudge, Rachel. "Girl, Unreconstructed: Why Girl Power Is Bad for Feminism." In Lisa Jervis and Andi Zeisler, eds., *BitchFest: Ten Years of Cultural Criticism from the Pages of* Bitch *Magazine*. New York: Farrar, Straus and Giroux, 2006, p.157

Heywood, Leslie, and Jennifer Drake, eds. *Third Wave Agenda: Being Feminist, Doing Feminism*. Minneapolis: University of Minnesota Press, 1997, pp. 2–3.

Hochschild, Arlie Russell, with Anne Machung. *The Second Shift: Working Families and the Revolution at Home*. New York: Viking, 1989.

Jensen, Michelle. "Riding the Third Wave." *The Nation*, December 11, 2000.

Klein, Allison. *What Would Murphy Brown Do? How the Women of Prime Time Changed Our Lives*. Emeryville, CA: Seal, 2006, pp.189–193.

MacEwan, Valerie. "Better Than a Poke in the Ass with a Sharp Stick." Interview with Lily James. *PopMatters*, www.popmatters.com/books/reviews/h/high-drama-in-fabulous-toledo.shtml. Accessed March 25, 2008.

Maio, Kathi. *Feminist in the Dark: Reviewing the Movies*. Freedom, CA: Crossing Press, 1988, pp. 215–219.

Merkin, Daphne. "The Marriage Mystique." *The New Yorker*, August 3, 1998, p. 70.

Millman, Joyce. "Ally McBeal: Woman of the '90s or Retro Airhead?" *Salon*, October 20, 1997.

Orange, Michelle. "There Goes My Hero—Finally." *MediaBistro*, September 14, 2005.

Pozner, Jennifer L. "The (Big Lie): False Feminist Death Syndrome, Profit, and the Media." In Rory Dicker and Alison Piepmeier, eds., *Catching a Wave: Reclaiming Feminism for the 21st Century*. Boston: Northeastern University Press, 2003 pp. 31-56.

———. "Makes Me Wanna Grrrowl: Spice Girls' Pre-Packaged Power Speak Reduces Feminism to Skintight Soundbites." *Sojourner: The Women's Forum*, April 1998.

Press, Joy. "Notes on Girl Power: The Selling of Softcore Feminism." *The Village Voice*, September 23, 1997.

Reed, Jennifer. "Roseanne: A 'Killer Bitch' for Generation X." In Leslie Heywood and Jennifer Drake, eds., *Third Wave Agenda: Being Feminist, Doing Feminism*. Minneapolis: University of Minnesota Press, 1997, pp. 122–132.

Rose, Tricia. *Black Noise: Rap Music and Black Culture in Contemporary America*. Hanover, NH: University Press of New England/Wesleyan University Press, 1994.

———. "Hip Hop's Herstory." *News & Notes* (NPR), June 11, 2007.

Siegel, Deborah. *Sisterhood, Interrupted: From Radical Women to Grrls Gone Wild*. New York: Palgrave Macmillan, 2007.

Walker, Rebecca, ed. *To Be Real: Telling the Truth and Changing the Face of Feminism*. New York: Anchor Books, 1995.

Watson, Shane. "Single White Female." *Harper's Bazaar*, July 1998.

Zeisler, Andi. "What's the Deal, McBeal?" *Ms.*, August–September 1999.

Chapter 5

Baumgardner, Jennifer, and Amy Richards. *Manifesta: Young Women, Feminism, and the Future*. New York: Farrar, Straus and Giroux, 2000.

Douglas, Susan J. "We Are What We Watch." *In These Times*, July 1, 2004.

Friend, Tad. "Feminist Women Who Like Sex." *Esquire*, February 1994.

Hernández, Daisy, and Bushra Rehman, eds. *Colonize This! Young Women of Color on Today's Feminism*. Emeryville, CA: Seal, 2002.

Hogan, Ron. "*Beatrice* Interview: Jill Nagle." *Beatrice*, 1997.

Johnson, Angela. "Confessions of a Pop Culture Junkie." *off our backs*, May 1994.

Levy, Ariel. *Female Chauvinist Pigs: Women and the Rise of Raunch Culture*. New York: Free Press, 2005, pp. 139-155.

Lewis, Sarah Katherine. "Is Stripping a Feminist Act?" AlterNet, May 4, 2007.

Nagle, Jill, ed. *Whores and Other Feminists*. New York: Routledge, 1997.

Paul, Pamela. *Pornified: How Pornography Is Transforming Our Lives, Our Relationships, and Our Families*. New York: Times Books, 2005.

Peyser, Marc. "Spinsterhood Is Powerful." *Newsweek*, January 13, 2003.

Pozner, Jennifer. "Dove's Real Beauty Backlash." *Bitch: Feminist Response to Pop Culture*, no. 30, Fall 2005.

———. "The Unreal World." *Ms.*, Fall 2004.

———. "The WB v. Your Uterus." *Bitch: Feminist Response to Pop Culture*, no. 29, Summer 2005.

Roe, Amy. "The Calculated Assault of Suicidegirls.com." *Willamette Week*, March 19, 2003.

Sharpley-Whiting, T. Denean. *Pimps Up, Ho's Down: Hip Hop's Hold on Young Black Women*. New York: New York University Press, 2007.

Siegel, Deborah. *Sisterhood, Interrupted: From Radical Women to Grrls Gone Wild*. New York: Palgrave Macmillan, 2007.

Solinger, Rickie. *Beggars and Choosers: How the Politics of Choice Shapes Adoption, Abortion, and Welfare in the United States.* New York: Hill and Wang, 2001, pp. 4–6.

Wolf, Naomi. *Fire with Fire: The New Female Power and How It Will Change the 21st Century.* New York: Random House, 1993, p. 184.

Wood, Summer. "On Language: Choice." *Bitch: Feminist Response to Pop Culture*, no. 24, Spring 2004.

INDEX

ACKNOWLEDGMENTS

It's humbling and a little scary to be considered an authority on anything, so first off I'd like to thank Brooke Warner, Denise Silva, and past and present Seal Press staff for inviting me to write this book and join the remarkable scholars and feminists who have contributed to this series. I'm honored to be among them.

My agent, Jill Grinberg, is just lovely all around, and I can't thank her enough for making this project possible.

I have heard for years from friends and colleagues that Jennie Goode is a fantastic editor, and I was thrilled to have the opportunity to experience it myself. Even when time was tight—and it often was—she was a calming, steady presence always ready with both encouragement and thoughtful, spot-on editing.

So many thanks go to my wonderful, always-supportive colleagues at *Bitch*—Briar Levit, Debbie Rasmussen, Amy Williams, and Miriam Wolf. Further thanks go to former *Bitch* intern Fatemeh Fakhraie for her help with research. And the final thanks go to my husband, Jeff Walls, who graciously let me hog the Netflix account to watch old Barbra Streisand movies for a solid three weeks.

ABOUT THE AUTHOR

ANDI ZEISLER is the cofounder and editorial/creative director of *Bitch: Feminist Response to Pop Culture*, which began in 1996 as an all-volunteer zine with a circulation of three hundred and is now an internationally distributed quarterly magazine with a circulation of more than fifty thousand. Andi's writing on feminism, popular culture, and politics has appeared in numerous periodicals and newspapers, including *Ms.*, *Mother Jones*, *Utne*, *BUST*, the *Washington Post*, the *San Francisco Chronicle*, the *Women's Review of Books*, and *Hues*.

© Jeffery Walls

Andi speaks on the subject of feminism and the media at various colleges and universities around the country, and she is a frequent guest on radio talk shows. Along with *Bitch* cofounder Lisa Jervis, she edited *BitchFest: 10 Years of Cultural Criticism from the Pages of* Bitch *Magazine*. A New Yorker by birth and temperament, she lives in Portland, Oregon, with her husband and dog.

CREDITS

Chapter 1

"The Male Gaze" is from the Hulton Archive. © Getty Images. Photographer: Douglas Grundy.

Chapter 2

"For Your Country's Sake Today" poster is reprinted with permission from The National Archives and Records Administration, College Park.

Image of Lucille Ball and Desi Arnaz courtesy of Desilu, too, LLC. "I Love Lucy" still image is reprinted with permission from CBS Television.

The Ronettes glamour shot is from the Hulton Archive. © Getty Images.

Protesters at the 1968 Miss America pageant is from the Tamiment Library and Wagner Labor Archives, New York University, Bobst Library.

Chapter 3

Excerpt from Elana Levine, *Wallowing in Sex: The New Sexual Culture of 1970s Television* is reprinted courtesy of Duke University Press. © Duke University Press, 2007.

Song lyrics from "Housework," *Free to Be...You and Me*, by Marlo Thomas and friends. © Arista Records.

Virginia Slims advertisement, campaign from the 1960s. © Phillip Morris.

Chapter 4

Chapter 5

SELECTED TITLES FROM SEAL PRESS

For more than thirty years, Seal Press has published groundbreaking books. By women. For women. Visit our website at www.sealpress.com. Check out the Seal Press blog at www.sealpress.com/blog.

A History of U.S. Feminisms, by Rory Dicker. $12.95, 1-58005-234-7. A concise introduction to feminism from the late-19th century through today.

Yes Means Yes: Visions of Female Sexual Power and A World Without Rape, edited by Jaclyn Friedman and Jessica Valenti. $15.95, 1-58005-257-6. This powerful and revolutionary anthology offers a paradigm shift from the "No Means No" model, challenging men and women to truly value female sexuality and ultimately end rape.

Hellions: Pop Culture's Rebel Women, by Maria Raha. $15.95, 1-58005-240-1. Maria Raha, author of *Cinderella's Big Score*, analyzes women ranging from Marilyn Monroe to the reality TV stars of the twenty-first century in an effort to redefine the notion of female rebellion.

What Would Murphy Brown Do? How the Women of Prime Time Changed Our Lives, by Allison Klein. $16.95, 1-58005-171-5. From workplace politics to single motherhood to designer heels in the city, revisit TV's favorite—and most influential—women of the 1970s through today who stood up and held their own.

Cinderella's Big Score: Women of the Punk and Indie Underground, by Maria Raha. $17.95, 1-58005-116-2. A tribute to the transgressive women of the underground music scene, who not only rocked as hard as the boys, but also tested the limits of what is culturally acceptable—even in the anarchic world of punk.

Listen Up: Voices from the Next Feminist Generation, edited by Barbara Findlen. $16.95, 1-58005-054-9. A collection of essays featuring the voices of today's young feminists on racism, sexuality, identity, AIDS, revolution, abortion, and much more.